Status of Micro Level Planning in India

– by –

M. Thaha

2018

Daya Publishing House®

A Division of

Astral International Pvt. Ltd.

New Delhi - 110 002

First Published, 1993
Reprinted, 2018

ISBN: 978-81-7035-112-2 (Hardbound)

Publisher's note:

Every possible effort has been made to ensure that the information contained in this book is accurate at the time of going to press, and the publisher and author cannot accept responsibility for any errors or omissions, however caused. No responsibility for loss or damage occasioned to any person acting, or refraining from action, as a result of the material in this publication can be accepted by the editor, the publisher or the author. The Publisher is not associated with any product or vendor mentioned in the book. The contents of this work are intended to further general scientific research, understanding and discussion only. Readers should consult with a specialist where appropriate.

Every effort has been made to trace the owners of copyright material used in this book, if any. The author and the publisher will be grateful for any omission brought to their notice for acknowledgement in the future editions of the book.

Published by : **Daya Publishing House®**
A Division of
Astral International Pvt. Ltd.
– ISO 9001:2015 Certified Company –
4736/23, Ansari Road, Darya Ganj
New Delhi-110 002
Ph. 011-43549197, 23278134
E-mail: info@astralint.com
Website: www.astralint.com

Acknowledgements

This State-of-the Art report on micro level planning in India aims to have an insight into the process of micro planning, devolution of financial resources, plan implementation etc. across the country which it is presumed would give a proper feed back to all those concerned with micro 'evel planning. The importance of this study on the threshold of Eighth Five-Year Plan in which the whole country is proposed to be covered by micro level plans need not be emphasised.

For this nation wide study, we had to collect information from different states. The information presented in this volume has been mostly gathered through interviews of senior officers of Planning Commission, New Delhi, State Planning Boards, Planning and Development Departments of State Governments and also from Statements presented during the discussion. It is quite impossible to acknowledge individually all of them as it is a long list of persons. However, we wish to record gratitude to Shri Asoke Basak, Secretary to Govt. of Maharashtra, Shri S.V. Giridhar, Secretary to Govt. of Gujarat, Shri D.S. Samant, Secretary to Govt. of Rajasthan, Shri B.N. Tiwari, Secretary to Govt. of Uttar Pradesh, Shri D.K. Sharma, Director, Planning, Govt. of Himachal Pradesh, Shri G.V. Viswanath, Planning Commissioner, Govt. of Karnataka, Shri S. Narayanan, Secretary to Govt. of Tamil Nadu, Shri I.C. Kumar, Secretary, Govt. of Bihar and Shri Srinivas Rath, Special Secretary, Planning, Govt. of Orissa, who spared their valuable time and shared their experiences. I thank all of them for their invaluable help.

In this effort I have been assisted by Dr. D. Shanthudu, Mr. R.R. Hermon and Mr. Sridhar Seetharaman, colleagues from Centre for Micro Planning. Draft report was revised several times and this has increased the task of typing this report. Shri SGK Murthy and Shri M. Balaji have done the work cheerfully. I take this opportunity to thank them all.

This study was undertaken as a Research Project of National Institute of Rural Development, Hyderabad. I express my sincere thanks to NIRD for funding this project and granting me permission to publish the report.

Author

Contents

I

Micro Level Planning—Strategy and Approach

The process of planning broadly signifies the achievement of predetermined social and economic goals in both spatial and temporal contexts. It involves the deploying of various resources in terms of men, money, materials, organizations and technologies in the most efficient manner so as to obtain maximum results at minimum costs. The essential aims are economic growth with social justice, maximizing of work opportunities, self reliance, enhancing income, removing regional and class disparities, bringing up the very poor to above poverty level of living and, in sum, to improve the quality of life for the nation as a whole.

There are various approaches to achieve these goals. In our country also different models of development have been experimented. These have no doubt brought overall growth but the benefits of development have not been shared by different pockets equally and hence the result is lopsided regional development. Equitable distribution of the benefits of development between different regions and also among different sections of population is a big challenge. In order to tackle this situation the importance of planning at the micro level is being increasingly realised and advocated.

In view of the prevailing conditions in the country the significance of micro level planning[1] as a mechanism to ensure allround balanced development has been recognised from the very inception of planning process in the country and consistently advocated from one plan to another. In the First Five Year Plan itself, importance of micro planning at the district level within the frame of state plan was emphasised. However, the concept itself could not be concretised and consequently, the exercise of formulation of the First Five Year Plan was confined to the state Headquarters.[2]

The Second Five Year Plan went a step further in micro level planning and identified certain sectors and activities to be planned and executed at the district level.[3] These were: (1) Community Development and National Extention Programme; (2) Social Welfare Extension Projects; (3) Agricultural Production Programme and Allied Activities such as Animal Husbandry, Soil Conservation etc; (4) Development of Cooperatives; (5) Village and Small Industries; (6) Housing and Urban Development; (7) Programme for the Welfare of Backward Classes; (8) Primary and Secondary Education; (9) Health Units and Sanitation; (10) Land Reforms; etc. Inspite of this, the exercise of micro level planning during this plan period could not go beyond identifying activities which can be planned and implemented with advantage at the district level.

The Third Plan emphasised the importance of micro level planning and the states were suggested to draw up plans adopting blocks and districts as planning units particularly for sectors, like (1) Agriculture including Minor Irrigation, Soil Conservation, Animal Husbandry, and Dairying; (2) Development of Cooperatives; (3) Village Industries; (4) Elementary Education; (5) Rural Water Supply and Programme of Minimum Rural Amenities like Approach Road; (6) Works Programme for the utilisation of manpower resources in rural area.

During the Fourth Plan it was realised that due to prevalent practice of formulating plan at the state level the diverse conditions existing in different pockets in the states had been ignored. On analysing the past performance of the approach adopted in planning, the Planning Commission came to the following conclusions.[4]

(a) The wide disparities in the level of development existing between different areas and community groups within a state cannot be narrowed down unless the resources to be provided and the programmes to be taken up in each area or for each community are determined on the basis of a proper assessment of local problems and potentialities.

(b) at the same time the natural resource potentialities, infrastructural facilities and productive capacities existing in different areas cannot be properly assessed at the state level.

(c) execution of such development schemes which are formulated at the state level without considering their suitability to local conditions leads to inefficient utilisation of physical and financial resources;

(d) meaningful assessment of on-going schemes can be undertaken only at the grass root level with the active participation of local officials and the beneficiaries of schemes.

(e) proper phasing to ensure synchronisation of one programme with other related programmes cannot be attempted without working out the details of programmes at the ground level;

(f) measures for the utilisation of local resources for development purposes cannot be planned realistically except in the specific context of the needs, aspirations and the economic condition of the people and the level of performance of local institutions; and

(g) the deliberate steps required to be taken up to identify the growth centres and to provide/locate the facilities and services required to meet the growing needs of the villages lying in their hinterlands cannot be taken except at the district level through the analyses of the emerging trends in economic activities and the pattern of facilities and services already available.

It was, therefore, considered necessary to look in greater detail into the aspiration and requirements of specific local areas, communities and situations and take suitable measures for meeting these so as to take maximum advantage of local initiative, potentials, capacities and resources. Therefore, the states were urged by the Planning Commission to adopt area approach in planning to have a firm basis for planning at the state level.

It was also decided that keeping in view the prevalent situation micro level plans should be prepared at district level. It was at this level that data were available. Moreover, the district was the lowest territorial unit at which most of the departments had officials who could (with some training and reorientation) formulate schemes suitable to the local conditions. The district was also considered by far the most convenient level to ensure proper coordination of activities among different departments. Due to these reasons the Planning Commission recommended that the district should be adopted as the normal unit for integrated area planning at the local level. It was, however, emphasised that national and state priorities should be kept in view while formulating district plans and wherever necessary, these would be supplemented by regional, sub-regional, market area and block plans for specific activities or functions.[5]

In order to facilitate planning at the district level, it was found necessary to change the procedure for the allocation of central assistance which was tied to certain programmes leaving little scope for identifying schemes suitable to different pockets. This procedure was, therefore, revised and the states were empowered to evolve their schemes in the light of local experience. They were also given the freedom to introduce administrative and organisational innovations considered necessary. As the districts differed in their problems and potentials of development, the decision about the material, administrative and financial resources to be allocated to individual districts was left to the states to be decided on merits of each case.[6] These guidelines suggested that the District Plans would have to be conceived and presented as annual operational plans formulated with reference to a long term perspective of development. The plan formulation exercise had necessarily to be preceded by a careful assessment of the existing problems, potentials and levels of development of different sub-regions and the performance of the on-going programmes and schemes. The planning process to be adopted in the formulation of district plans were also specified.[7] The district officers incharge of different activities through analyses of the statistical tables had to list out the resources available, problems and prospects in different sectors setting-forth the priorities to be accorded to different activities.

This was, in fact, a preliminary framework for evolving sound strategy for the development of districts. They would then discuss with the officials and non-officials at the block and district level the proposals contained in the plan framework and obtain their views. The block/district level officers' views about role played by cooperatives, panchayati raj bodies and other institutions in the provision of services, participation in plan formulation and programme implementation and raising of local resources could also be ascertained. Experience of implementing different programmes could also be discussed in order to understand the administrative or other problems hindering the implementation process. The BDOs out of their field experience were in a position to make suggestions for projecting the demand for agricultural inputs such as fertilisers, seeds, pesticides, tractors and also credit for the above items as also for minor irrigation and rural electrification. They could also explain the possibility of raising local resources for village roads, school buildings, location and opening of high schools and colleges, and the augmentation of medical facilities. The sectoral officers were also directed to consult progressive farmers and entrepreneurs to ascertain their views about the problems or activities need to be taken up on priority basis in different areas. Discussions were also to be held with the representatives of the cooperatives, local self-government bodies, banks and PR institutions to get a feed back on the preliminary framework and to assess the quantum of resources likely to be available for the district plan. In the light of those discussions, the draft had to be revised and discussed with the district level officers individually. Subsequently, in a general meeting of all the district level officers, guidelines for drawing up detailed schemes for inclusion in the district plan had to be arrived at. The district level officers had to formulate their schemes keeping in view those guidelines and specifying (a) the objectives, (b) the activities envisaged, (c) the financial, physical and personnel inputs required, (d) the physical results expected from year to year, (e) the quantum of private and institutional resources likely to become available towards its execution, and (f) the manner in which the scheme would be reviewed, coordinated and synchronised with other schemes and evaluated from time to time. The schemes so formulated had to be presented in the form of an integrated and operational plan.

The process of district planning envisaged as above in the guidelines of the Planning Commission was a mere recommendation and the state governments had the freedom to adopt or modify it according to their need. Consequently most of the states could not work out these modalities and hence micro level plans could not be prepared.[8] Therefore, it was felt necessary that the state level planning machinery should be strengthened to take up this responsibility. Keeping this in view, the Planning Commission launched a scheme for strengthening of the regional/district planning unit in the State Planning Departments with "competent and qualified" technical staff.

Since the Fifth Five Year Plan amelioration of poverty, unemployment and social inequality received greater attention and became central theme of various development programmes. In order to deal with these situations it was felt necessary to bring down the mechanism of planning and decision making to levels where they can come to grips with the people and their problems and where they can organise an appropriate package of programmes/activities with a measure of active community support. At this stage, block level planning was conceived to complement the rural development effort through fuller utilisation of local resources for full employment on the one hand and a quick attention to the local problems on the other. It was thought that a development block would be an ideal unit for planning and implementation of programmes as the blocks are sufficiently small in terms of area and population to enable intimate contact and understanding between the planners, those responsible for implementation of the plan and the people.[9] It also provides an observation platform in close proximity to the beneficiary group and thus helps to:

i. understand more clearly the felt needs of the people and factors inhibiting the upliftment of the weaker sections;
ii. ascertain area (block) specific physical and human resource potential;
iii. identify constraints inhibiting socio-economic and technological growth; and
iv. expand the area of people's participation in the preparation and implementation of plans.

Recognising the importance of blocks as a planning unit, in November 1977, the Planning Commission appointed a Working Group under the Chairmanship of Prof. M.L. Dantwala to draw up guidelines for block level planning. The working group suggested that plan for the block should be integrated on the one hand to the plans of the districts and the state levels and on the other hand to the plans for the sub-units comprising of clusters of villages within the block. The working group also arrived at the activities which could be planned and executed at the block level without sacrificing planning efficiency. These include: 1. Agriculture and allied activities; 2. Minor irrigation; 3. Soil Conservation and Water Management; 4. Animal Husbandry; 5. Fisheries; 6. Forestry; 7. Processing of Agricultural Produce; 8. Organising input supply, credit and market; 9. Cottage and Small Industries; 10. Local infrastructure and 11. Social services which include—a. Drinking water, b. Health and Sanitation, c. Education, d. Housing, e. Sanitation, f. Local Transport, g. Welfare programmes.

The working group also noted that the pattern of staff available for planning purposes at the district and block levels, both quantitatively and qualitatively, was quite inadequate. While at the district level there was some staff for planning, at the block level even this was absent. Therefore, the group recommended that expertise was required for taking up the task of (a) preparation of resource inventory and analysis; (b) project formulation and appraisal; (c) manpower planning and budgeting; (d) monitoring and evaluation; and (e) credit planning.

The working group was also of the opinion that it would be necessary to have specialists in the fields like agronomy, industry and engineering. Therefore, it was recommended that the district level planning machinery should be strengthened and entrusted with the responsibility of formulation of block plans. The minimum core staff suggested for this professionally qualified team consisted of (1) Chief Planning Officer, (2) Economist/Statistician (Project formulation and evaluation) (3) Cartographer/Geographer, (4) Agronomist, (5) Engineer (Irrigation/ Civil); (6) Industry Officer (small and cottage industries) (7) Credit Planning Officer.

The financing of the block level planning had to depend on the devolution of financial resources from the state. Therefore, state plan outlays were proposed to be classified into divisible and non-divisible outlays. The divisible part of the state plan had to be allocated to the districts. Out of the allocations received by the districts, there was a further distribution among schemes proposed to be implemented at district level and for those schemes forming part of the block level plan. The principles of resource transfer from the state to the district and from district to the block level were left to be evolved in a manner acceptable to states.

The objective of the block planning was also considered as achieving equity in the distribution of goods and services to all the villages. Therefore, for taking locational decisions for different socio-economic infrastructure facilities 'spatial planning'[10] was suggested. Standards for spatial distribution of facilitis were also suggested and operational guidelines for block level planning were also formulated by the Planning Commission in 1978-79. It was suggested that the different phases of planning should be completed within a period of six months.

As a result of all these efforts, block level plans were prepared in the country but the scope of these plans was limited to IRD programmes and these were not comprehensive development plans by any standard.

The experience gained in the country in more than 30 years of planning demonstrated that micro level planning has to be backed up by sound practice.[11] The capabilities for decentralised planning have to be built up, the right procedures and suitable structures have to be evolved and necessary technical and administrative changes, have to be brought about. Therefore, during the Sixth Plan period, the Planning Commission had undertaken some ground work for these changes. The procedures for effecting functional, financial and administrative decentralisation to the districts were outlined to the states. A Central scheme of strengthening the Planning machinery at the district level on a sharing basis was launched. Training programme on 'District and Block level planning' were organised under a Central Scheme administered by the Department of Personnel (Training Wing).

In June 1982 Planning Commission addressed the states, urging them to take steps towards four important aspects of decentralised district level planning set up. These were interalia:

a. Effecting functional decentralisation—it included identification of the exclusive functions that must be planned and implemented at the district level. This procedure was expected to help in defining the role of district planning in the multi-level planning structure.
b. Effecting financial decentralisation—this was necessary to make the district planner clearly aware of the funds likely to be available for district development.
c. the establishment of appropriate planning mechanism at the district level—this included the setting up of District Planning Board/Council with appropriate composition, and strengthening of the planning machinery at the district level.
d. Establishment of appropriate budgeting and reappropriation procedures.

The above measures were emphasised by the Planning Commission in the context of the formulation of the Annual Plans with the result that many states took steps to disaggregate, district-wise, divisible outlays of the state plans and introduced corresponding administrative decentralisation measures.

The working group on District Planning set up by the Planning Commission in September 1982, advocated a gradual step-by-step approach towards the goal. It suggested that PRIs wherever they exist would function as the apex body to approve as well as review the implementation of district plans. Where the PRIs either did not exist or existed without planning functions, the District Planning Boards/ Councils which were already or being constituted, could perform these functions. In this task they were to be assisted by a suitable planning machinery at that level. In view of this, the centrally sponsored scheme of strengthening of state level planning machinery was extended to district level also with effect from 1982-83.

In spite of all these efforts as observed in the Seventh Plan, sufficient arrangements were not made in the organisation of technical and administrative personnel at the state level and below to facilitate decentralisation. The lack of adequate machinery for decentralised planning and administration thus continues to be a critical weakness in the existing system. But, with the introduction of a variety of new programmes for rural development requiring close coordination with other departmental programmes in the rural areas, the need for decentralisation of planning and development administration to the district and block levels has become all the more imperative.

While emphasising district as a unit for planning during the seventh plan, it has been suggested that eventually the decentralisation of planning should be extended further to the block level, particularly for the effective implementation of anti-poverty programmes. Various measures are being adopted by the Planning Commission to make further progress in the task of micro level planning. As the deficiency in the existing machinery for micro level planning is quite clear, the existing scheme of strengthening of the district planning machinery is being continued during this plan also.

As it is evident, technical know-how for the formulation of micro level plans available in the country at lower levels is quite inadequate and therefore, there is a need to undertake large scale training programmes on micro level planning. Keeping this in view the Government of India have sponsored a number of training programmes for imparting training to the trainers in district planning who in turn would train the officers incharge of micro level planning in different states. Guidelines for designing the training programme in district planning have also been formulated and issued to the state governments. The Planning Commission has also undertaken an exercise to assess the training needs in micro level planning of different target groups and identifying the institutions wherein such training can be imparted. The state planning secretaries have been urged to organise training on this subject in the selected institutions within the state. A task force on training needs in district planning has also been set up for assessing the training needs and working out the strategy to achieve it.

The Planning Commission also envisages providing technical guidance to the states by initiating a few pilot projects on district planning to improve methodology and procedure for plan formulation. For this purpose, to start with, five districts in different states have been selected for formulation of Pilot district plans. These districts are: Tirunelveli Kattabamam (Tamil Nadu), Nashik (Maharashtra), Munger (Bihar), Sitapur (U.P.), Shimla (Himachal Pradesh). Technical guidance for plan formulation in these pilot projects are being provided by the National Institute of Rural Development, Hyderabad.

Besides these projects, at the instance of the Planning Commission, in another eight states altogether 17 districts have been selected for the formulation of pilot district development plans (Table 1.1). The State Governments have been made responsible for formulation of plans for these pilot projects.

During the current plan, Government is making efforts to strengthen the data base for natural resource inventory at the district level through use of remote sensing techniques. In this country, about 100 districts have been selected for this purpose. Detailed land use maps are being prepared under this project for different districts. Besides, the use of computers in micro level planning is also being emphasised. The Department of Science and Technology has taken up a project called Natural Resources Data Management System (NRDMS) to develop computer compatiable methodology for collation, storage, analysis and retrieval of data on natural resources and socio-economic parameters. Through this project, methodology for generating upto-date resource inventories for micro level planning is also being developed. Currently this methodology is being operationalised through district level data base in a few selected areas. So far, data bases in five districts have been set up. These are: Sultanpur (U.P.) Visakhapatnam (A.P.) Khera (Gujarat), Koraput (Orissa), and Gurgaon (Haryana). In these districts, Mini Computer Systems have been set up. It is expected that by the end of the Seventh Plan, 23 districts will be covered under this project.

Table 1.1
States and Districts Selected for Pilot Projects in District Planning

States	*Districts*
1. Andhra Pradesh	a. East Godavari
	b. Adilabad
	c. Anantapur
2. Assam	a. Nalbari
3. Bihar	a. Munger
	b. Purnea
	c. Ranchi
4. Himachal Pradesh	a. Shimla
	b. Mandi
	c. Kangra
5. Jammu & Kashmir	a. Dist. in Jammu division
	b. Dist. in Srinagar Division
6. Karnataka	a. Kolar
	b. Mysore
	c. Dharwad
	d. Raichur
7. Kerala	a. Kottayam
	b. Cannanore
8. Maharashtra	a. Nashik
9. Uttar Pradesh	a. Jhansi
	b. Hardoi
	c. Sitapur.

The Study

Against this background, at the anvil of the Eighth Five Year Plan it is felt appropriate to look into the progress made by different states in operationalising the micro level planning concepts. It is evident that the priorities assigned by different state governments vary considerably consequently the states are at different stages in micro level planning. The assessment of the current status of micro level planning in different states will indicate the task ahead in operationalising this concept and in turn enable the policy makers to evolve strategies for promoting it further. With this intention the present study has been taken up and the broad objectives are: (1) to review the strategy and approach adopted for micro level planning in different states in terms of functional and financial decentralisation for plan formulation; (2) to examine the machinery available for undertaking plan formulation, implementation and monitoring at the micro level; (3) to assess the task ahead in operationalising micro level planning, and the concomitant policy implications.

As the basic objective of the study is to assess the status of micro level planning in different states, it was necessary to gather information from state level as well as from lower tiers. The information has been gathered primarily from secondary sources through discussions held with the Secretaries and Deputy Secretaries to Government of Planning Department, Directors of Planning, Directors of Department of Statistics, District Collectors and District planning officers. The discussions were centred around different aspects of micro level planning as prevalent in the states. The aspects covered were organisational set up, responsibility of planning team, coordination among the planning team and other sectoral departments, process of plan formulation, implementation and its monitoring, allocation of divisible fund, availability of untied funds/ discretionary grants, power of reappropriation etc. Obviously relevant literature available on the subject were also utilised.

The study has been presented in six chapters. The chapter on Strategy and approach traces the genesis of micro level planning and highlights the efforts made by Central and state governments over different plan periods to operationalise the concept. In the subsequent chapters, status of different aspects of micro level planning across the states have been presented which starts with the review of planning machinery or organisational arrangement for taking up the task of formulation and implementation of micro level plans. Constitution of these organisations along with their roles have been described. This is followed by a chapter on functional decentralisation for micro level planning which presents the so designated district/block/mandal level schemes which are to be planned and implemented at the local level. The next chapter has been devoted to the subject of devolution of financial resources as adopted by different states. This would help to understand the freedom enjoyed by the authorities at the local level in implementing their plans. The next chapter synthesises the process of planning adopted in different states to evolve micro level plans. All the above referred aspects of micro level planning have been summed up in the last chapter and projected for policy implications.

Notes and References

1. The term Micro Level Planning refers to formulation of "integrated area development plans" for smaller areas starting from a village upto a district.
2. Lal, Tarsem. District Development Planning, A case study of Two districts, Concept Publishing Company, New Delhi, 1986, p. 44.
3. Planning Commission, Second Five Year Plan, 1966, pp. 156 and 158.
4. Planning Commission, Guidelines for the Formulation of District Plans, 1969, pp. 2-4.
5. Planning Commission, op. cit., p. 6.
6. Ibid., pp. 1-2.
7. Planning Commission, op. cit. pp., 15-28.
8. Tarsem, op. cit., p. 63.
9. Planning Commission Report of the Working Group on Block Level Planning, 1978, pp. 4-5.
10. Spatial planning implies a systematic effort to locate facilities like roads, schools, factories, houses etc. in relation to human settlements where all people can use them to maximum advantage. Such convergence can effect large economies in movement of men and materials and better utilisation of facilities.
11. Planning Commission, Report of the Working Group on District Planning, Vol. 1, 1989, p. 21.

II

Planning Machinery

Availability of institutional infrastructure for shouldering the responsibility of plan formulation and implementation is an important pre-requisite for micro level planning. Even though in recognition of the necessity for proper institutional infrastructure a scheme to strengthen it was launched as early as in the Fourth Five-Year Plan, still the states are at different stages and have adopted varying patterns. Therefore, an attempt is made in the following pages to take stock of the institutional infrastructure available in different states.

In spite of the prevailing diversity in the arrangements, there are some common features in the structure of planning machinery. This common feature is the existence of two agencies at the district level in most of the states responsible for plan formulation. One agency plays mainly an advisory role, whereas the other one is an executive body and hence technical in nature. The advisory body has different nomenclatures in different states like District and Review Development Board/District Planning Board/District Planning and Development Committee/District Planning and Development Council, etc. These are high power bodies at the district level involving top level officials and elected representatives of the people in the district. In some states it is the district Collector who is the Chairman of this body whereas in other states, a Minister of the state cabinet is its Chairman. This body considers the district plans formulated by the District

Planning Organisation. It may suggest changes in the plan, projects/ programmes subject to the availability of resources, suggest changes in the priorities and finally approve the plan.

In discharging the duties, the Planning Board/Council is assisted by Executive Committee which consists of a limited number of officers who have a key role in the formulation and implementation of the plans. The executive committee is assisted by the planning cell at the district level which is mainly responsible for the formulation of plans. In some cases there are task forces or expert groups to provide technical assistane to the executive committee and in turn to the planning board/ committece at the district level.

There is also a planning board/commission at the state level responsible for the formulation of overall policy, issues and guidelines for plan formulation. These policies and guidelines are transmitted to units at district and lower levels. By and large, the state level machinery has a supervisory role. The status of planning machinery existing in different states is discussed below:

ANDHRA PRADESH

With the constitution of District Development Boards in 1984, a beginning was made for decentralisation of planning process in Andhra Pradesh. Later, in 1987, this system was changed and a two tier system at district and Mandal level was introduced. At the district level as many as 17 organisations/institutions are associated with the planning and implementation of various development programmes. (Table 2.1)

District Development Review Board

District Development Review Boards (Zilla Abhivruddi Sameeksha Mandali) have replaced the Zilla Development Boards in all the districts except Hyderabad (urban) in February 1987. The Chairman of the Board is a state Minister nominated by the Chief Minister, all MLAs and MPs of the district and a few individuals who have major contributions in development/planning/social service are also nominated by government. The Chairman, Zilla Praja Parishad is its Vice-Chairman and District Collector is member-secretary. The DDRB with all the District Administrative Machinery under its control is mainly responsible for approval, sanction and review of plan and non-plan schemes implemented in the district. The specific functions of DDRB are:[1]

Table 2.1

District Level Organisations Associated with Planning and Implementing Development Programmes in Andhra Pradesh

1. Zilla Praja Parishad;
2. Mandal Praja Parishad;
3. Municipalities/Corporation;
4. District Rural Development Agency;
5. S.C. Service Coop. Finance Corpn;
6. S.T. Finance Corporation;
7. I.T.D.A;
8. Dist. Level Committee on Women Welfare;
9. A.P. State Housing Corpn;
10. Society for Training and Employment Programmes (STEP);
11. Handicapped Welfare Corpn;
12. Minorities Corporation;
13. Dairy Development Corporation;
14. Forest Development Corporation;
15. Agro Industries Corporation;
16. A.P. Irrigation Dev. Corporation;
17. A.P. State Rural Dev. Corpn.

(a) to consider and make recommendations for accelerated development of the district as a whole encompassing rural and urban areas and to ensure balanced regional development.

(b) to help formulate district development plans for all departments other than local bodies.

(c) to indicate inter-sectoral priorities to the government for allocation of funds to different schemes implemented by various agencies at the district level.

(d) to allocate funds, received from the state government among the various implementing agencies (excluding Zilla Praja Parishad) in the district keeping in view the guidelines issued by the government from time to time and also to accord administrative sanctions for individual schemes to be taken up from out of the funds so allotted.

(e) to supervise, review and monitor the implementation of all the developmental schemes (both plan and non-plan) at the district level of all the development departments including the corporate bodies.

The district development and review board is assisted by the Chief Planning Officer in performing its task of reviewing and monitoring the development work. The Chief Planning Officer along with the skeleton staff provided to him work under the control of District Collector. There is a proposal to strengthen this technical cell by appointing experts on spatial planning, credit planning, project appraisal, social development and computer programming.

Zilla Praja Parishad (ZPP)

Under the new structure of the Panchayati raj set up, the Zilla Praja Parishad is another body constituted at the district level. The Chairman, Zilla Praja Parishad is directly elected by all the voters in the district excluding those residing in Municipal areas. All the Mandal Praja Parishad Presidents who are elected in the lower tier of P.R. system (Mandal) are the members of Zilla Praja Parishad. In addition, some members from Minorities and Women are co-opted as members. The District Development Officer (DDO) who is the Chief Executive of Zilla Praja Parishad is a middle level IAS officer or a Senior level officer of Panchayati Raj department. The engineering and education departments constitute two important wings of Zilla Praja Parishads. These wings look after rural water supply, rural roads, Minimum Needs Programme, NREP and RLEGP schemes and secondary level education. Some of the above schemes are implemented directly by Zilla Praja Parishad engineering wing and a few through Mandal Praja Parishads. The ZPP has jurisdiction over the entire rural area in the district and exercises full administrative and fiscal powers over the Mandal Praja Parishads. It also coordinates and consolidates the plans prepared for Mandals, secure execution of plans, projects and schemes and other work related to mandals. The ZPP functions through six standing committees constituted out of its members, with each committee assigned certain subjects.

District Rural Development Agency (DRDA)

This agency deals with the rural development programmes. The staff of DRDA include Assistant Project officers in the fields of

Agriculture, Animal Husbandry, Industries, Monitoring besides a Project Economist. The Project Director is the Chief Executive of DRDA and the District Collector is the Chairman. The DRDA has a Governing body which includes Zilla Praja Parishad Chairman and MLAs, MPs, district level heads of development departments and a few others nominated by the Government as members. The governing body normally meets once in a quarter to approve the action plans and review the performance periodically. The programmes implemented by District Rural Development Agency include IRDP, TRYSEM, Drought Prone Areas Programme etc. All these programmes are implemented either through the Mandals or line departments like agriculture, animal husbandry etc.

Corporations

To look after the welfare of certain specified groups like scheduled castes, scheduled tribes, minorities, women and youth state government has established various corporations.[2] At district level there is a unit to implement the programmes of the respective corporation in liaison with various other concerned departments. The scheduled caste cooperative societies look after the economic development of scheduled caste households in the district by providing the required inputs and credit. The District Collector is the ex-officio Chairman. The Executive Director of the society formulates the society's plan consisting of schemes like community irrigation wells, assigned/surplus land development, social forestry, bonded labour, rehabilitation, training programmes, individual schemes etc. and implements through the Mandals and line departments.

Similarly there is S.T. service cooperative society which implements the programmes for the economic development of ST households in the district in association with the concerned departments. Where there is a large concentration of S.T. population exclusive agencies are formed to look after the allround development of STs including infrastructure development like roads, education etc.

On the same lines for the economic development of backward classes at district level, B.C. service cooperative society has been established. The District Backward classes welfare officer is the ex-officio Executive officer and Collector is the ex-officio chairman.

For the welfare and economic activities of women in the district also a district level committee on women's welfare headed by the District Women's Welfare officer has been created with District Collector as the ex-officio chairman.

There is also SC & ST Housing Corporation which deals with the Housing programme for SC/ST/BCs and other weaker sections at the district level. The Collector is the Executive Director of the Corporation and District Manager the Chief Executive. This agency constructs the houses for the weaker sections by providing loan and subsidy. The loan is drawn by the State Government from HUDCO and commercial banks. The beneficiaries construct the houses on their own under the supervision and guidance of the officials of Housing Corporation.

A Society for Employment and Training have also been formed at district level with a view to developing skills in various trades and to provide self employment opportunities for the unemployed youth. The Chief Executive Officer will function under the Chairmanship of the District Collector. There is also a Minorities Corporation with a coordinator to look after the economic development of minorities.

All the above mentioned societies/agencies are not having any field staff. Their plans and programmes are prepared and implemented with Mandal as a unit by the Mandal staff.

Line Departments

In addition to the above mentioned institutions there are development departments functioning under the direct supervision and control of the respective departments. The policies and programmes of these departments are finalised at state level and the district officers and the field staff at sub-district level implement the programmes as per the guidelines of the respective state heads of departments. But at district level their activities are supervised by the Collector. Some of the programmes of line departments are directly implemented by the departmental staff whereas a few others mainly beneficiary oriented programmes of line departments are implemented through mandals.

Financial Institutions

The credit needs of the people are met by cooperative and commercial banks through their branch network. The District

Cooperative Central Bank which draws funds from state cooperative bank distributes loans to the farmers through their Primary Agricultural Credit Societies (PACS). The functioning of Commercial Banks and cooperative banks is monitored by a district level committee of bankers. The committee meetings are chaired by the District Collector. The Lead Bank officer drawn from the leading bank of the district assists the Collector in this task of monitoring.

Mandal Praja Parishads

Below the district level the Mandal Praja Parishads have been constituted replacing the panchayat samithies. A Mandal is a group of 10-25 villages covering a population of 25 to 40 thousand. The President of MPP is directly elected by all the voters of the Mandal. The Mandal Development Officer (MDO) is the Chief Executive.

The staff of the Mandal include an Education Officer, an Engineering Officer and a Cooperative and Rural Development Officer, besides 2 to 3 Village Development Officers each one covering 5 to 10 villages.

The important subjects/programmes implemented by the Mandals are Primary and Upper Primary Education, Drinking Water Supply, Approach Roads, Minor Tanks, Rural Development, Housing and other weaker sections' beneficiary oriented programmes, NREP/RLEGP, Social Forestry etc. The Mandal Praja Parishad is thus the supreme authority in so far as the local development works are concerned.[3]

It is a nodal agency for execution of all the developmental programmes of Zilla Praja Parishad, different corporations, and line departments.

ASSAM

In this state micro level planning has been introduced in all the plain districts from 1986. Sub-divisions which are the next lower level administrative units below the districts, have been taken as a unit for planning and sub-divisional Planning and Development Councils have been constituted at this level as an advisory body. However, the technical exercise of plan formulation for the sub-divisions is done at the district level by the Core-Group (Executive Committee). There is also a Decentralised Planning Division at the state level which plays a supervisory role in micro level planning for the sub-divisions in the state. For the Hill Districts, the arrangements are slightly different and District Councils have been constituted for these areas.

Sub-Divisional Planning and Development Council

As mentioned above at the level of sub-division, in all the 16 districts in the plain there are sub-divisional planning and development councils. Each council is headed by a Minister of State Cabinet with Deputy Commissioner as its Vice Chairman and Additional Deputy Commissioner (Development) as member-Secretary. All the MLAs and Chief of Executive Councils or Mahkama Parishads of the sub-Division are its members (Table 2.2). The Divisional Commissioner has been nominated as alternative chairman in the council so as to ensure an important role from him in the sub-divisional planning process. Representatives from the lead bank are included in the council to facilitate coordination and integration of the credit plan with the development plan. The representative of the State Planning and Development Department who is also a member of the council provides on behalf of the department on the spot explanations, clarifications etc. required by the council.

Table 2.2
Composition of the Sub-Divisional Planning and Development Council in Assam

1.	Cabinet Minister	Chairman
2.	Divisional Commissioner	Alternate Chairman
3.	Dy. Commissioner	Vice-Chairman
4.	Dist. planning officer (at present ADC-Dev.)	Member-Secretary
5.	Sr. Planning officer	Jt. Secretary
6.	Sub-divisional officer	Member
7.	All members of the parliament of the sub-divisions	Member
8.	All members of the legislative assembly of the sub-division	Member
9.	Chief Executive Council or the Mahkama Parishad of sub-divisions	Member
10.	Secretary, Mahuma Parishad of the sub-divisions	Member

(Contd.)

11.	Chairman of the municipalities/town committees of the sub-divn.	Member
12.	Dist. officers of the Dev. dept	Member
13.	Dist. officers of the Dev. department	Member
14.	Project Director, DRDA	Member
15.	Sub-divisional officer of the sub-divisions	Member
16.	Two economists from research institutions/ universities/colleges	Member
17.	Two social workers	Member
18.	One representative from the lead bank of the sub-divn.	Member
19.	One representative from the State Planning & Dev. Dept.	

The Sub-Divisional Planning and development council has been constituted as an umbrella organisation for each sub-division and functions as an advisory body. It finalises the development plans of the sub-division, monitors and reviews the progress of the plan implementation and allocates departmental outlays. The council also approves sites of different projects/schemes and list of beneficiaries at this level.

District Level Core Group

Besides the Council at the sub-divisional level, at the district level a core group which is perhaps equivalent to the executive committees in other states has been constituted as a technical body under the chairmanship of the Deputy Commissioner, with District planning officer (presently ADC—Development) as Vice-Chairman. Other members of the core group are Sub-Divisional officer, Sub-Divisional Planning officer and Project Director (DRDA) Senior Planning Officer is the Member-Secretary.

The main function of the core group is to prepare draft sub-divisional plan. It also scrutinises the operational plan, prepared and submitted by the district heads of development departments on the basis of the financial allocation made for the sub-division, for placing it before the Sub-Divisional Planning and Development Council for approval. The Core Group also reviews the progress of implementation of the operational plan and suggests measures for removal of difficulties if any, faced by implementing departments.

Planning Cell

Although sub-divisions are the units for planning the planning cells have been proposed to be set up at the district headquarters, with the following staff for each district.[4]

1. Addl. Dy. Commissioner (Development)
2. Senior Planning Officer
3. Asst. Planning Officers (two)
4. Research Assistants (two)
5. Upper Division Assistant
6. Lower Division Assistant

State Level Decentralised Planning Division

At the state level a decentralised planning division has been created ur ler the state planning and development department. This division is headed by a Director drawn from IAS cadre. He is assisted by one Joint Director, Sr. Research Officer; Research Officers; Assistant Research Officers (four each) and eight Research Assistants. The main functions of the state level planning division are:[5]

1. formulation of policies, procedures and guidelines for preparation of sub-divisional plans and evolve methodology for the same;
2. to work out norms for distribution of funds among the sub-divisions and fixation of size of the annual sub-divisional plan;
3. to work out norms for distribution of funds at the sub-divisional level for different sectors of development and fixing the same;
4. coordination with administrative departments in matters relating to sub-divisional planning;
5. monitoring of the progress of implementation of sub-divisional plans;
6. organisation of training of officers of the state government in multi-level planning; and
7. to take up studies relating to micro level planning and evolve methodology thereto.

BIHAR

Micro level planning has been introduced in this state since 1985-86. District has been taken as the unit for planning and therefore, the institutional infrastructure for micro level planning are mainly confined to this level. Like other states, in Bihar also there is a policy making body known as District Planning and Development Council. DPDC is assisted by Executive Committee which deals with formulation, implementation and review of district plans. Besides, there is a small district planning cell. The overall supervision and guidance for all these institutions is provided by the state planning commission.

District Planning and Development Council (DPDC)

In pursuance to the state government policy of decentralisation of planning and development efforts, district planning and development council has been constituted under the chairmanship of a minister nominated by the Chief Minister (Table 2.3). Other members of the District Planning and Development Council are the Divisional Commissioner—Vice Chairman, Chairman of the Zilla Parishad—Member, Collector of District (Member Secretary), the Deputy Development Commissioner (Additional member secretary), all members of the state legislature and parliament elected from the district, the Chairman of District Central Cooperative Bank, a representative of District Lead Bank, all Pramukhs of the Panchayat Samithies of the District, an Economist from the university service and the Chairmen or Mayors of the Municipalities/Corporations in the district. The District Planning Development Council (DPDC) is envisaged as a policy making body.

The DPDC formulates draft Annual plans for the District sector schemes on the basis of the ceiling of allocations and other guidelines issued by Government. Besides plan formulation, the DPDC and its Executive Committee review and monitor progress of execution of development schemes in the district. DPDC meetings are held bi-monthly for transacting these business.

Executive Committee

The DPDC is assisted by an executive committee at the district level headed by Divisional Commissioner. Other members of the executive committee are the District Magistrate (Co-Chairman), the District Development Commissioner (Vice-Chairman), the District Planning

Officer (Member Secretary), the sectoral heads, and a representative of district lead bank. The executive committee plays a very pivotal role as it fixes the priority, goals and objectives of development at the district level. The committee also scrutinises the financial estimates of different schemes proposed in the Annual Action Plan according to the needs.

District Planning Cell

A district planning cell consisting of a District Planning Officer and other technical and ministerial staff has been created.[6] The cell's main responsibility is to scrutinise the plan estimates proposed by the departments.

Table 2.3
Composition of Divisional Planning and Development Council in Bihar

1.	Minister (nominated by Chief Minister)	Chairman
2.	Divisional Commissioner	Vice-Chairman
3.	District Collector	Member-Secretary
4.	Deputy Development Commissioner	Addl. Member-Secretary
5.	All members of the state legislature and parliament elected from the district	Member
6.	The Chairman of District Central Cooperative Bank	Member
7.	A representative of District Lead Bank	Member
8.	All Pramukhyas of P.Ss of the district	Member
9.	Economist from the university service	Member
10.	Chairman or Mayor of the municipalities/ corporations in the district	Member
11.	Chairman of the Z.P.	Member

State Planning Commission

Bihar State Planning Commission has been constituted under the chairmanship of the Chief Minister. Other members of the State

Planning Board are the Development Commissioner (Ex-officio Deputy Chairman) the Chief Secretary of the State Government (Member). All Development Commissioners of sectoral departments such as Agriculture, Industries, Infrastructure and social welfare (members) the Finance Secretary (member) Planning Secretary (Ex-officio Member-Secretary) at the state level. The State Planning Commission deals with the policy matters and provides overall guidance to different institutions on district planning.

GUJARAT

Gujarat is one of the few states in the country which has made some strides on micro level planning. In this state, panchayati raj system introduced two decades ago, is now well established.[7] The taluka level planning committee has emerged as an institution providing a link between the gram panchayats and the District Planning Boards. The DPB which is the apex institution for micro planning at the district level is assisted by the Executive Planning Committee and also sub-committee on Employment Generation formed at the district level.

Taluka Level Planning Committee

Even though Gujarat has long history of micro level planning, until recently, no separate planning machinery existed below district level. During 1984 a planning committee at the taluka level was constituted. This committee comprises of taluka President, the Taluka Development Officer (TDO) Medical Officer (P.H.C.) Deputy Executive Engineers, President of Social Justice Committee, President of Nagar Panchayat, the MLA/MP of the area, and members of the district panchayat. The TDO is generally the convenor of this committee which usually meets once in three months for reviewing progress. The committee also finalises the schemes received from the Gram Panchayats and forwards it to the district planning officer for approval of the district planning board. Proposals received from the Gram panchayats regarding the NREP works are examined and sanctioned by the Deputy Executive Engineer who is a member of the committee. He is assisted by a Junior Engineer.

Every taluka has one E.O. (IRDP) for planning and execution of IRDP. He is supported by 10 VLWs each in charge of a cluster of villages. The E.O. works under the supervision of the T.D.O. The block/taluka level organisation is currently in the process of being strengthened. Four posts of E.O. (Credit, Animal husbandry, industry and women and child care) have been sanctioned and are in the process of being filled up. A post of E.O. (Stat.) has also been sanctioned in talukas covering more than two blocks.

Most of the taluka level decisions regarding IRDP are made in Taluka Level Coordination Committee (TLCC) which meets once in a month. The TDO is the convenor of this committee and the meeting is attended by bankers, E.O's and VLWs and an APO from DRDA.

District Planning Board

The emphasis on decentralised planning has led to the establishment of District Planning Boards (DPB) as early as in 1973 at district level. These boards which function as planning bodies were reconstituted in 1980 in all the districts and have a varied and highly representative character. Originally President of District Panchayat was made Chairman of DPB. Later Collector was made the Chairman and currently a Minister functions as Chairman, the Collector its Vice-Chairman and the District Panchayat President its co-vice-chairman. All MLAs, MPs, representatives from Panchayati raj bodies, municipalities or municipal corporations, representatives from credit institutions, research workers and a member of the State Planning Board as well as the Planning Department are represented in the DPB (Table 2.4).

District planning boards have been charged with a number of responsibilities concerned with planning, implementation and evaluation of development programmes. These are —

(i) Preparation of district development plan;

(ii) Formulation of specific schemes in different sectors to be funded from the outlays available under decentralised planning.

(iii) Ensuring maximum participation from local bodies, industrial houses, public and voluntary agencies in the formulation and implementation of the plan;

(iv) Undertaking a regular and effective review and evaluation of all the district level schemes and strive to remove bottlenecks and take remedial measures for the successful implementation of these schemes.

(v) Monitoring and evaluation of the minimum needs and beneficiary oriented programmes.

(vi) Identifying difficulties in the implementation of the schemes and take up the matter at the appropriate level to remove such difficulties.

(vii) Identification of infrastructure gaps for the family oriented programmes and formulation of appropriate schemes for filling up these gaps.

Table 2.4

Composition of District Planning Boards

1.	A Minister of State Government	Chairman
2.	District Collector	Vice-Chairman
3.	President of the Dist. Panchayat	Co-Vice-Chairman
4.	Taluka Panchayat Presidents of two or three talukas of the District (two for small Districts and three for large Districts)	Member
5.	All MLAs elected from the district	Member
6.	All MPs elected from the district	Member
7.	President of one of the Municipalities in the district	Member
8.	Mayor of the Municipal corpn.	Member
9.	Municipal Commissioner	Member
10.	The President of the Nagar Panchayats of the district	Member
11.	An expert from a Research Institution	Member
12.	A representative of the district Lead Bank	Member
13.	Chairman District Central Cooperative Bank	Member
14.	District Dev. Officer	Member
15.	Project Administrator Tribal Area Sub-Plan	Member
16.	A Member of the State Planning Board	Member
17.	Chairman of a Social Justice Committee of the District	Member
18.	A lady Member of Zilla Panchayat (to be nominated by Zilla Panchayat)	Member

(Contd.)

19.	District Planning Officer	Member-Secretary
20.	Dist. Statistical Officer	Addl. Member-Secretary
21.	Officer of the G.A.D. (Planning Division)	Observer

In discharging these duties, as mentioned earlier, the District Planning Board is assisted by Executive Planning Committee and sub-committee on employment.

Executive Planning Committee

The Executive Planning Committee headed by the Collector is a compact committee of eight or nine members (Table 2.5). It has a representative character built into it by the inclusion of the MLAs from the district who are appointed by rotation. The Executive Planning Committee meets every month. The functions of this executive planning committee are: to monitor the implementation of the schemes sanctioned by the DPB. It also examines and scrutinises every scheme before submitting it to the DPB; to ensure that it is in accordance with the guidelines issued by the government. The sub-committee for employment generation is headed by the Collector and has the District Development Officer as Vice-Chairman. It deals with manpower and employment requirements at the district level.

District Planning Team

Each District Planning Board has been provided with a small complement of staff headed by a District Planning Officer, who is a Class-I officer drawn from the Gujarat Administrative Service/Gujarat Statistical Service/Gujarat Agriculture Service. He works under the direct supervision of the Collector. The D.P.O. is assisted by a Research Officer, a Research Assistant, a Deputy Mamlatdar, two Statistical Assistants and a sub-Auditor. The District Planning Team has the responsibility of monitoring the projects financed by the District Planning Board as well as the projects taken up under the Minimum Needs Programme (MNP). In order to ensure effective monitoring of MNP projects, one Research Assistant and a Statistical Assistant have been appointed exclusively for this purpose.

Table 2.5
Composition of Executive Planning Committee in Gujarat

1. District Collector	Chairman
2. President of the Dist. Panchayat	Co-chairman
3. Three MLAs of the Dist. (appointed by rotation)	Member
4. Dist. Dev. Officer	Member
5. Project Administrator, Tribal Area sub-plan	Member
5. Dist. Planning officer	Member-Secretary
7. Dist. Statistical officer	Addl. Member Secretary

HIMACHAL PRADESH

The state government, in principal, has accepted the decentralisation of planning process in the state and ground is being prepared for the formulation of micro level plans at the district level.[8] As a step towards operationalising the micro level planning in the state the District Planning and Development Committees and Executive Body have been formed as an apex body in 10 out of 13 districts. Further, district planning teams have been constituted to assist the DPDC.

District Planning and Development Committee

This is the apex body concerned with planning and development at district level. The main function of this committee is to oversee the programme implementation by different departments through monitoring and review. The DPDC is a powerful body as evident from its composition. (Table 2.6).

The DPDC has a small executive body to assist in transacting its functions, with Deputy Commissioner as Chairman and Additional Deputy Commissioner as the Member Secretary. All heads of offices are its members.

District Planning Cell

In this state, planning cells have also been constituted with a limited contingent of staff. There are: (a) ADC/ADM/Chief Planning Officer, (b) Research Officer/Economist, (c) Credit Planning Officer, and

(d) Technical Assistant. The planning cell functions under the supervision of Deputy Commissioner. As in the case of DPDC the planning cell's main responsibility is monitoring and evaluation of schemes, implemented in the district.

The specific responsibility of the planning team are[9]—

(1) Compilation of progress reports received from the departments. (2) Holding quarterly meetings to monitor progress of plan schemes implemented in the district. (3) Preparation of indicators of development which include: (i) demographic indicators, (ii) agro-economic indicators, and (iii) infrastructural indicators. (4) Preparation of resource inventory and data base for district planning which includes (i) Physical resources, (ii) Human resources, (iii) infrastructure, and (iv) institutions to monitor the physical and financial aspects of development (5) to maintain inventory of funds for programme implementation in the district. (6) to maintain the list of schemes executed under the drought relief (7) to conduct evaluation and ad-hoc studies as per requirement of the state government from time to time. (8) to make on the spot inspection of execution of plan schemes in the district.

Table 2.6

District Planning and Development Committee Set Up in Himachal Pradesh

1. Minister	Chairman
2. Chairman of Zilla Parishad (wherever these exists)	Vice-chairman
3. Deputy Commissioner of the district	Co-chairman
4. All Members of Parliament, from the district	Member
5. All the Members of Legislative Assembly from the district	Member
6. Chairman, Block Development Committee	Member
7. Representatives of Women organisation/ to be nominated by the state government	Member
8. Representatives of voluntary organisation	Member
9. Representatives of Urban Local Bodies	Member
10. Representatives of Khadi and Village Industries Board	Member
11. Representatives of Financial Institutions	Member
12. A.D.C./A.D.M.	Member-Secretary

JAMMU AND KASHMIR

The Jammu and Kashmir state has the distinction of being amongst the first few states in the country to introduce micro level planning.[10] In early sixties on a pilot basis district level planning was introduced in Ladakh district with single line system of administration. Consequent upon the success of this arrangement the state government in 1976 took a decision to extend micro level planning to other districts of the state and since 1986 District Development Boards have started functioning in all the districts in the state. Micro level planning has taken long strides in this state and now blocks have been taken as the basic unit of planning. However, till such time a machinery capable of formulating and implementing plans at block level comes into existence this function is being performed by the District Planning Machinery which assists the DPB.

District Development Board

In all the districts in this state, there are District Development Boards and the District Development Commissioner, has been assigned the role of Chief Coordinator as the Chairman of the DDBs. A unique feature of the DDB in this state is that the Superintending Engineer of the district has been made Vice Chairman of DPB. Besides, all MLAs and MLCs of the district, one elected Sarpanch from each Block Development Board of the district and representatives of weaker sections, backward areas and women nominated by the government are also members of DDB. Deputy Director Planning (Statistics) is the Member Secretary of the DDBs. The board has been conceived as a local authority with blend of administrative capability and planning expertise. The District Development Commissioner is overall incharge of the development of the district and exercises powers of major Heads of Departments in respect of development departments functioning in the district. All such departments in the district have been placed under his administrative and operational control. The administrative approvals, technical and financial sanctions of the schemes to be implemented at the district level are vested with the district Development Commissioner and the Superintending Engineer of the district.

The DDB enjoys that rare privilege of power to determine plan priorities for the district development. The DDB also guides the formulation of development plans for the district. The DDB is responsible to ensure speedy development and economic upliftment of the people of the district. The Board periodically reviews the progress and achievement of developmental plans and schemes in operation and makes such recommendations as it considers appropriate. The Board also functions as a working group for the formulation of periodic and annual plan for the district.

The DDB meets atleast three times in a year. The first meeting is generally held in the beginning of the year for formulation of the annual plan. The second meeting is held for the mid term appraisal of the plan and third meeting is usually held to review the performance of the annual plan at the close of the year.

District Planning Cell

A Planning Cell has also been provided at each district to assist the district development board in the formulation and implementation of the plan. The cell is headed by an officer of the rank of Deputy Director (Planning). It is proposed to strengthen these cells by induction of subject matter specialists like credit planner, agronomist, social development officer and land development officer. The district planning cell assists the District Development Commissioner in the formulation, implementation and monitoring of the district plan.

District Statistical Agency

At the district level there is a statistical agency which conducts sample surveys and coordinates the data flowing from different departments in the district to the state headquarters. The agency also brings out the District Statistical Hand Book once in two years which contains among other things the resource inventory of the district which is required for plan formulation.

KARNATAKA

Micro level planning at the district level in the state of Karnataka was introduced in the Fifth Plan with the establishment of District Planning Committees. Later, in 1978-79, Mandal Panchayats and Zilla Parishads were established. Thereafter, keeping in view the concept of decentralisation in administration from April 1, 1987 Mandal Panchayats were also taken as a unit for planning. Thus, micro level plans are being prepared at the Mandal Panchayat as well as at Zilla Parishad levels. In Karnataka the developmental functions have been completely bifurcated and the District Collector is concerned with only revenue and law and order functions.

Mandal Panchayat

A Mandal Panchayat covers a revenue village or a group of villages having a population of not less than 8,000 and not more than 12,000. However, in the districts of Chickmangalur, Dakshina Kannada, Kodagu, Shimoga and Uttar Kannada a population of 4000 has been accepted as the minimum to constitute a mandal. Each such mandal has a mandal panchayat. A mandal panchayat comes into existence on the notification of a declaration by the Collector and all its members are elected. The mandal panchayat elects two members to be Pradhana and Upapradhana. Seats in Mandal panchayats are reserved for women, backward classes, scheduled castes and scheduled tribes. A Mandal panchayat performs three distinct functions, usually described as obligatory, discretionary and transferred functions. Obligatory functions include construction, repair and maintenance of roads, drains, bunds, regulation of grazing lands, lighting of the villages and so on. Discretionary functions include such work or measure which promote the health, safety, education or general well being of the people. Transferred functions are those assigned by the government, i.e. management of forests, waste land, cultivation of common lands etc. Mandal panchayats also plan and execute the schemes pertaining to these sectors. The Mandal panchayat has a full time Secretary (of the rank of an extension officer) appointed by the Zilla Parishad in consultation with the mandal panchayat.

Zilla Parishad

Since district has been adopted as the unit of local administration, it is at this level that organisational support and technical competence are available for planning, supervision and coordination of development programmes. Due to these reasons the Zilla Parishad at the district level has emerged as the most powerful unit of planning and development in Karnataka state. The jurisdiction of this democratic executive agency extends over the entire district excluding areas included in a Municipality or a Municipal Corporation. The Zilla Parishad consists of elected members, associated members, as well as nominated members. In the Z.P. there are elected members from taluka for each twenty eight thousand population or part thereof except for the hilly tract of Kodagu

(Coorg) district where a member represent a population of twelve thousand or part thereof. The Chairman of the District Central Cooperative Bank is an Associate Member. He is entitled to take part in the meetings of the Zilla Parishad but cannot vote. Nominated members of Z.P. are members of Parliament, Members of Legislative Assembly and of Legislative Council. Only such MPs and legislators who represent whole district or a part thereof and whose constituencies lie within the jurisdiction of the Zilla Parishad are members of Z.P. Those MLCs who are not elected from territorial constituencies but are resident of the district are entitled to participate in the proceedings and to vote. A Zilla Parishad has an Adhyaksha and an Upadhyaksha elected from among the members. They hold office for a period of five years the same term as that of members. The Chief Executive Officer of Z.P. is known as 'Chief Secretary'. He is of the rank of a Deputy Commissioner of a district. The Chief Secretary supervises and controls the execution of works and developmental schemes and also draws and disburses money out of the Zilla Parishad funds.

Being the most important body of the new panchayati raj set up, the Zilla Parishad has planning, executive, advisory as well as monitoring powers.[11] The Act also stipulates it obligatory on the part of Zilla Parishad to make reasonable provisions for overall supervisions, coordination and integration of development programmes.

Standing Committees

All the activities of the Zilla Parishad are being implemented through standing committees which are in fact Executive Committees. These are: General, Finance and Audit, Planning and Development, Public Works and Amenities, Social Justice, Education, Agriculture and Animal Husbandry, Health and Industries standing committees. Each committee is also assigned a specific responsibility in the area indicated by the name of the committee. Among them, the most important one the social justice committee has a mandate to promote educational, economic, social and cultural interests of SCs, STs and backward classes and to protect them from social injustice and all other forms of exploitation. Each committee has a maximum of six members elected from amongst members of Zilla Parishad. The Chief Secretary of the Zilla Parishad is the ex-officio secretary of the standing committee

KERALA

In this state, micro level planning is in its infant stage.[12] All the sectors are planned under the supervision of the directors/heads of departments concerned, at the state level. It is proposed to decentralise the planning process in Kerala in a phased manner and some organisational arrangements have been made to take up this task.[13] District Development Councils (DDCs) at the district level and Block Development committees at the block level have been constituted. District planning Committees and sectoral planning committees have been also set up. There is also District Advisory Committee for Scheduled Castes. The District Annual Plan is placed before this committee for advice prior to its finalisation. This committee also reviews the implementation.

The establishment of district planning units at the district in 1979 was a major step towards decentralised planning. The district planning officer who heads the unit is a senior officer of state service or drawn from Indian Administrative Service. He is assisted by a Deputy Planning officer and a Statistical Assistant. The district planning unit deals mainly with the formulation and implementation of schemes under the special component plan.

District Development Council

Pending the enforcement of Kerala District Administration Act of 1979 the State Government have given the responsibility of plan formulation at the district level to the District Development Council (DDC). The District Collector and his staff would assist the DDC. It is also considered necessary to have representative bodies at the district, block and panchayat levels to facilitate planning from below. It is expected that this requirement will be fulfilled partly by the DDC at the district level, block development committee at the block level besides the elected panchayat bodies at the panchayat level. Three sub-committees on 1. Agriculture and allied sectors, 2. Industry and infrastructure 3. Social services are also proposed. As planning is essentially a technical exercise it has been decided that the main brunt of the plan formulation has to be borne by the technical personnel of various departments at the district, block and panchayat levels. At the same time the decision is to associate all other existing agencies including public sector, local self-government and panchayat with the task of planning and implementation of development programmes.

Working Groups

In each district working groups have been constituted with District Collector as Chairman, District Planning officer as Secretary and District Welfare Officer, Asst. Development Commissioner and nominated officers of other development departments as Members.[14] Each Head of the Department has nominated district level officer of the department who is responsible for formulating the scheme under the Special Component Plan of that department. The working group also has the representatives of agencies like Kerala State Electricity Board, Kerala State Development Corporation for Scheduled Castes, Scheduled Tribes etc. The working group acts as catalysts in expediting decisions and helping in fixing locations for different proposed institutions such as schools, dispensaries etc. In respect of schemes like electrification the working groups are to play the role of advisers. The working group is also empowered to sanction economic development schemes costing upto Rs. 10 lakhs.

District Planning Unit at State Level

The first exercise on planning from 'grass-roots level' was attempted in this state in 1978 by the State Planning Board which has a separate unit on district planning. This unit has a Chief (District Planning) Assisted by one Deputy Director, Assistant Directors and Research Assistants. This unit has a compilation of basic data pertaining to each district required for plan formulation. This unit is also charged with the responsibility of preparation of resource inventory and formulation of model district plans.

MADHYA PRADESH

In Madhya Pradesh, like in many other states, efforts are on to operationalise the concept of micro level planning. It is to be noted that the decision to decentralise the planning process in this state was taken as early as 1973 and District Planning Boards were constituted in all the 45 districts in the state. These District Planning Boards underwent several changes since then and in its present form were reconstituted in 1980.[15] The District Planning Groups and the District Planning Cell assist the DPB. There is no institutional infrastructure below the district level.

District Planning Board

The District Planning Boards in the state of Madhya Pradesh are unique in the sense that its chairmen are nominated by the State Government from out of the three prominent social workers nominated earlier as members of the District Planning Board. The District Collector is the Secretary of the Board and the District Planning Officer its Deputy Secretary (Table 2.7).

Table 2.7
Constitution of District Planning Boards

Chairman	Nominated by the State Government from amongst the three nominated social workers of the districts
Secretary	The District Collector
Deputy Secretary	The District Officer
Members	1. The President of the Dist. Panchayat.
	2. All Members of Parliament from the district.
	3. All Members of Legislative Assembly from the district.
	4. The President of the biggest urban local body.
	5. The Chairman of the Dist. Land Dev. Bank.
	6. The Chairman of the Dist. Coop. Bank.
	7. The Manager of the Lead Bank of the district.
	8. All Presidents of Janapad Panchayats.
	9. Three prominent Social workers of the district, one of them has to be a woman.

The DPB is expected to carry out the following functions:

1. To analyse the district's material and human resources, identify local resource-based projects, determine their priorities and formulate development plan for the district.
2. to effectively coordinate the development efforts of the various agencies, organisations and departments functioning at the district level.
3. to ensure maximum participation and help of local bodies and people from different strata of society in the formulation and implementation of the plan programmes.

4. to monitor plan projects, schemes and programmes to ensure effective implementation thereof.
5. to undertake selective evaluation studies in order to provide appropriate feedback to the planning department and the implementing bodies at the district and state levels.
6. to ensure timely recovery of government and cooperative dues so that financing the plan is not affected.

District Planning Committee

The District Planning Board is assisted in its working by a District planning committee consisting of all important district heads of development departments working under the Chairmanship of the Collector (Table 2.8).

Table 2.8
District Planning Board

Chairman	The Collector of the District
Secretary	The District Planning Officer
Members	1. The Chief Executive Officer of District Panchayat
	2. The Deputy Director of Agriculture
	3. The Asst. Registrar Cooperative Societies
	4. The Divisional Engineer (Electricity)
	5. The Divisional Forest Officer
	6. The District Industries Officer
	7. The Executive Engineer (Irrigation)
	8. The Executive Engineer (PHE)
	9. The Executive Engineer (PWD)
	10. The Dy. Director Animal Husbandry
	11. The District Statistical Officer
	12. The Asst. Director Fisheries.

District Planning Unit

With a view to carrying out the planning exercise at the district level more scientifically and actively and to assist the District Planning

Committees and the District Planning Boards in the proper discharge of their functions, the district planning units have been constituted. The District Statistical Officer in addition to his normal duties also functions as the District Planning Officer in the district planning unit. He is assisted by District Credit Officer and Statistical Officer.

MAHARASHTRA

Maharashtra has introduced micro level planning since the beginning of the Fifth Five-year Plan. In all the 30 districts of the state, District Planning and Development Councils have been constituted which are assisted by the Executive Committees and District Planning Cells. Overall guidance for formulation of district development plan is being provided by the State Level Planning Department. Planning at the block level has also been introduced in this state as pilot projects.

District Planning and Development Council

For each district, District Planning and Development Council (DPDC) has been constituted with the functions of formulation, monitoring and approval of district plans and bringing about coordination between various implementing agencies at the district level. The DPDC consists of representatives of the people from the district, representatives of urban and rural local bodies, various development corporations set up by the State Government in addition to 14 non-official members nominated by government from persons who have knowledge and experience of socio-economic pursuits. The designated minister of the district (Palak mantri) is the Chairman of the DPDC. The Commissioner of the division is the Vice-Chairman and the Collector is the Member-Secretary. Members elected to the Lok Sabha and Vidhan Sabha as well as members of Rajya Sabha and Vidhana Parishad residing in the district are also its members. President and Chief Executive officer of the Zilla Parishad, representatives (one each) of (A), (B) and (C) class municipal councils, mayors of municipal corporation, municipal commissioner and representatives of the District Central Cooperative Bank, Land Development Bank, Lead Bank, Regional Development Corporation, State Khadi and Village Industries Board etc. are also members of this body.

Executive Committee

The DPDC mainly operates through its executive committee and the special executive committee for the Tribal Area sub-Plan. The executive committee is headed by the designated Minister of the State and it is a compact body. It has all powers of the DPDC and can discharge all functions of the DPDCs. Government have also appointed a special executive committee of DPDCs for tribal area sub-plan for all the 14 districts covered under the sub-plan. The designated Minister of the district is the Chairman and tribal commissioner is the Vice-Chairman of the committee. One of the elected representatives who is a member of tribal community from the district is also the Vice-Chairman of the special executive committee.

District Planning Cell

All the activities of the DPDC are carried out through the District Planning cell. The Planning cell consists of District Planning Officer (drawn from Directorate of Economics and statistics of the rank of Deputy Director working under the planning department of the state), two research assistants one statistical assistant, two economists, three supporting staff (Clerk-cum-Typist), and one peon. The District Planning cell's major role is compilation and scrutiny of the plans received from different departments and to assist the Collector in monitoring of the plan implementation.

ORISSA

Micro level planning is being operationalised at the district level in this state and since 1979 serious attempts have been made to achieve it. In this state the apex advisory body for micro planning at the district level is the District Development Board, whereas the District Planning Committee is the executive body assisted by the District Planning cell.

Planning Boards are in existence in all the districts in this state. The Board has an advisory role in plan formulation and also ensures participation of people's representatives and the public in the formulation and implementation of development programmes. The Board is headed by a designated minister as its Chairman and the M.P. of the district is Vice-Chairman. The District Collector is the Member Secretary of the Board (Table 2.9). The specific responsibilities of the board are:

(1) to formulate broad guidelines, based on the availability of funds, for the formulation of sectoral plans at the district level.

Table 2.9
Composition of District Planning Board in Orissa State

1. Designated Minister	Chairman
2. M.P. of the district	Vice-Chairman
3. District Collector	Member-Secretary
4. One nominee from DPC	Member
5. Revenue Divisional Commissioner	Member
6. 8 MLAs	Members
7. 4 Panchayat Chairman	Members
8. 2 experts in the field of agriculure, industries, irrigation etc. from the district	Members
9. Representative of local voluntary organisation	Member
10. Executive Director, family welfare	Member
11. Chairman of notified area council	Member

(2) to guide the district planning committees in the preparation of resource inventories and identification of backward pockets/ areas suffering from infrastructural deficiency;

(3) to advise the district planning committees in the selection of appropriate programmes in various sectors and their inter-sectoral coordination and integrated into comprehensive district plans;

(4) to finalise the draft district plans framed by the district planning committees.

District Planning Committee

In 1984 a decision was taken by the State Government to create suitable planning machinery at the district level capable of drawing up "Integrated District Plan". As a result the District Planning Committee (DPC) came into existence.[16] The Collector is the Chairman of DPC. The other officers in the district representing various development departments such as Agriculture, Cooperation, Forest, Animal Husbandry, Education, Health and Family Welfare, Harijan and Tribal Welfare, Public Works, Industries, Irrigation, Fisheries, Employment and Statistics are members. Assistant Director (Dist. Plan) incharge of planning cell acts as member-secretary of the District Planning committee.

The District Planning Committee's responsibility is to analyse the district's resources, identify local resources based projects, determine their priorities and draw up district plans i.e. perspective five-year and annual plans as part of the state plan. In this effort they are required to integrate the development efforts of different agencies, organisations and departments functioning at the district level. The district plans would also have to be integrated with the sectoral plans. The DPC is also supposed to evolve suitable procedures for formulation of the block plans for incorporation into the district plan. Besides, it is required to monitor and simultaneously review the implementation of selected important schemes and projects. Selective evaluation studies are also to be undertaken by DPC in order to provide appropriate feed back to state planning department, concerned government departments, heads of departments and implementing agencies. DPC is also required to undertake studies on manpower planning and employment generation at the district level.

Subject Matter Working Groups

In order to make indepth studies, subject matter working groups are set up by the district planning committee, under the chairmanship of the concerned highest subject matter specialist/officer who is a member of the district planning committee. The concerned medium level specialist of the district planning cell acts as its member-secretary. Where a medium level specialist is not available, the Assistant Director (District Plan) acts as the member-secretary of the working group. Members of the working group are nominated by the Collector. Keeping in view the expertise and relevance to the subject tasks are assigned to the working group in consultation with the chairman of the concerned group and approved by the district planning committee. The working groups meet as often as their assignments require and/or as may be directed by the chairman of the DPC. At present 17 working groups are functioning at the district level for reviewing the progress of various development programmes (Table 2.10).

District Planning Cell

As a first step towards decentralised planning in the state, the district was taken as the lowest unit and action was initiated to create a suitable

Table 2.10
Illustrative list of Subjects on which Working Groups are Set up in the District of Orissa

S. No.	*Subjects*	*Chairman*	*Officer of Dist. planning cell to act as member secretary*
1	2	4	5
1.	Agriculture, crop husbandry horticulture, soil conservation	Dy. Director Agriculture	Agriculture specialist
2.	Cooperation, agriculture marketing, storage and warehousing	Dy. Registrar Cooperative societies	Credit planning specialist
3.	Rural development poverty amelioration programmes including NREP, RLEGP etc.	Dy. Registrar Cooperative societies	Credit planning specialist
4.	Irrigation, Minor (Flow & lift) dug wells	E.E. (Minor irrigation)	Engineering specialist
5.	Animal husbandry and dairy development	Chief district veterinary officer	Agriculture specialist
6.	Fisheries Fisheries	Asst. Director (Dist.Plan)	Asst. Director
7.	Command area development	Project Director, CADA	Engg. specialist
8.	Rural electrification, energisation of pumpsets, alternative energy sources	E.E. OSEB	Engineering specialist
9.	Industries including Technical education and craftsman training	GM DIC	Asst. Director (Dist. Plan)
10.	Mineral Development	Dy. Director Mines (incharges)	Engineering specialist

(Contd.)

1	2	4	5
11.	Communication including roads, road transport, inland water transport	E.E. (R & B)	Social services specialist
12.	Elementary education, secondary education, adult education and functional literacy programme, physical education, sports and literacy.	Inspector of schools	Social services specialist
13.	Health and Family Welfare	DMO	-do-
14.	Drinking water supply	EE (Public health	-do-
15.	Welfare of SC/ST	Collector	Asst. Director (Dist. Plan)
16.	Social welfare housing	DDO	-do-
17.	Manpower and employment	Collector	Cartography specialist
18.	Afforestation and social forestry	DFO	

planning machinery at this level for drawing up a need and resource based integrated district plan. On the basis of recommendations of the working group of Planning Commission, a planning cell (Dist. planning unit) was set up to take up preliminary planning exercises in regard to district plan formulation. This planning cell has been created with one Asst. Director (Dist. plan), two senior Economic Investigators, and one Cartographer. The cell which functions under the direct control of the Collector, coordinates the plan formulation activities and interacts with the various plan executing authorities at the district level and prepares suitable data base on resource inventories for the plan formulation purposes. The unit is supposed to undertake selective monitoring and evaluation of programmes as may be considered necessary for getting appropriate feed back for effective implementation of development programmes.

RAJASTHAN

Although the state government has accepted in principle the concept of micro-level planning, only some rudimentary steps in this direction have been so far possible in Rajasthan.[17] From the beginning of Fifth-Plan for meaningful involvement of the local people's representatives in the process of planning for MNP components, District Planning Committees were set up in each district. The State Government now propose to establish District Planning Councils and District Planning Units to operationalise the concept of micro level planning.

District Planning Committee

The district planning committee constituted in the beginning of the Fifth plan has since been reconstituted into a full-fledged district planning committee in each district under the chairmanship of District Collector. Its membership is extended so as to cover all the district level officers. This committee is now the main agency at the district level responsible for planning, coordination of developmental activities and to oversee implementation of plan programmes. This committee has been assigned the following tasks.[18]

1. to lay down long term as well as short term strategy for development and formulate guidelines for preparation of integrated district plan, keeping in view the directions issued in this respect by the state government;
2. to assess the resource potential of the district;
3. to effect coordination between the various development plan programmes within the district.
4. to monitor the progress of implementation of plan programmes in the district.
5. to ensure local cooperation in the implementation of approved programmes wherever necessary.
6. to formulate proposals in regard to sectors covered under minimum needs programme in accordance with the guidelines issued by the state government.

District Planning Council

It is now proposed to have a new body of District Planning Council with Minister incharge of the district (to be nominated by the

Government) as Chairman. The day to day functions of district planning would be looked after by a District Planning Executive Committee to be set up separately. To provide necessary administrative/official support, separate district planning cells would be created with necessary technical support in addition to that already available at the district level.

UTTAR PRADESH

The Government of Uttar Pradesh took a dynamic step towards the reorientation of the planning process and introduced the system of micro level planning during 1982. In this state districts have been taken as the unit for micro level planning and institutions to be concerned with formulation of these plans have been constituted at the district, division as well as state level with different roles.

District Planning and Monitoring Committee

In every district, district planning and monitoring committee has been constituted under the chairmanship of a Member of the Council of Ministers (Table 2.11). This committee is the apex body at district level concerned with matters of development and is empowered to order an enquiry into any matter, that it deems fit

Table 2.11
Constitution of the District Planning and Monitoring - Uttar Pradesh

1.	A member of the Council of Ministers	Chairman
2.	All members of Parliament from the district	Member
3.	All members of state legislature from the district	Member
4.	District Magistrate	Member
5.	Chief Development officer/Additional District Magistrate (Development)/District Development officer	Member Secretary

The committee is empowered (1) to finalise the plan of the district keeping in view the guidelines issued by the state government as well as the plan outlays earmarked for the district; (2) to allocate departmental outlays between various blocks on the basis of norms prescribed by the State Government from time to time to eradicate disparities; (3) to review both state sector as well as district sector schemes incorporated in the district plan; (4) to submit proposals for reallocation of funds, received from the district plan, and (5) to obtain periodical reports from various departmental officers as and when needed.

District Plan Coordination and Action Committee

This committee assists the district planning and monitoring committee in discharging its responsibilities. District Magistrate is the Chairman of this committee and all district level officers of development departments are its members. The Chief Development Officer or Additional District Magistrate (Development) or District Development Officer is the Secretary. The District Economic Officer (Leader of the planning team) functions as Joint Secretary of this committee. The committee is entrusted with the task of (a) formulation of district plan for submission to district planning and monitoring committee for finalisation, (b) monthly review of the plan progress, and (c) to put up proposals for reallocation of funds to district planning and monitoring committee.

Executive Committee

The Executive committee at the district level is called 'Pariyojana Rachnavam Abantan Samithi'. The District Magistrate is the Chairman and CDO/ADM (D)/DDO as well as District Departmental Heads and a representative of the lead bank in the district are its members. The Executive committee's responsibility is to arrange for institutional finance for Integrated Rural Development programme and other schemes. It also ensures coordination between various schemes of district as well as state sector so as to avoid duplication of effort. The executive committee also sends proposal to district planning and monitoring committee for financial and administrative approval.

District Planning Team

It consists of one Economic Officer with two Assistant Economic Officers and one Cartographer. The team assists the District Magistrate in plan formulation and monitoring at the district level.

Divisional Level Committee

At the divisional level there is a committee for reviewing and approving the district plans and forwarding it to state government for final approval. Its role is advisory as well as administrative as all officers of development departments at the Divisional level are its members. Commissioner of the division is Chairman. All District Magistrates of the division are its members and Joint/deputy development commissioner is member-secretary.

State Level Committee

The state level committee comprising of secretaries of departments of planning, finance and administrative departments has been constituted to look into the sectoral plans of the district and make necessary changes in the plan.

WEST BENGAL

In West Bengal micro level planning in its present form has been introduced from 1985-86.[19] Districts and blocks have been taken as units for micro planning. The institutional infrastructure has also been created at these two levels. At the block level there is a block planning committee whereas at the district level there are two bodies—one is a deliberative and approving body, designated as the district planning and coordination council (DPDC) and the other executive arm of DPDC which is known as the district planning committee. These district and block level planning committees are assisted by standing committees.

Block Planning Committee

The block planning committee has been constituted at the block level with the Karmadhyakshas of the Sthayee samitees (standing committees), Pradhans of Gram Panchayats, block level officers of all departments and block development officer as the member-secretary.

District Planning Coordination Council

At the district level there are deliberative and approving body designated as the District Planning and Coordination Council (DPDC) with the Minister hailing from the district as the Chairman and District Magistrate as Member-Secretary. Other members of the DPDC are 'Sabhadhipati'. Zilla Parishad, Sabhadhipatis of all panchayat samities, chairmen of Municipalities, MLAs, MPs, and district level officers of Government Departments. Divisional Commissioner is a permanent invitee of the council.

District Planning Committee

The District planning committee is the executive arm of the DPDC and functions as the actual planning agency. The district planning committee is constituted with the District Magistrate as the Member-Secretary. 'Karmadhyakshas' of the Asthayee Samities of the zilla parishad, Sabhadipatis of all panchayat samithies, Chairmen of the Municipalities in the district, one representative of each of the statutory bodies in the district, district level officers of all departments in the district have also been enrolled as the members of district planning committee. Sub-divisional officers of the district are the permanent invitees and district level officers of the banks would be invited as and when necessary.

Standing Committees for Planning and Development

At the Zilla Parishad as well as the panchayat samithi level there are standing committees for planning and development (Parikalpana-o-Unnayan Asthayee samithi). These committees undertake the resource survey and assist in formulating plan for the district and block sector schemes.

State Planning Board

Like other states, West Bengal also has a planning machinery at the state level which is designated as Planning Board which helps and guides the DPCs and BPCs and the state departments in formulating and implementing the plans. The State Planning Board also undertakes the exercise of continuous appraisal in addition to the monitoring done by various authorities at various levels.

A close look on the preceding pages on the institutional infrastructure availability at different states in the country leads to the conclusion that the states have succeeded in making some arrangements for planning at the district level in most of the states. In some of the states at sub-divisional, block and mandal levels, process of micro level planning has been started. The long list of functions and powers assigned to different advisory bodies as well as executive and technical units reflect only the importance of these institutions. But these institutions have to go a long way to have the technical capabilities to discharge the duties assigned to them in the most fruitful way.

Notes and References

1. Rao, Y, Venkateswara, Machinery for Planning, Multilevel Planning in India, Process and Perceptions Ed. Reddy, Y. Venugopal, Centre for Economic and Social Studies, Hyderabad, 1988, pp. 36-37.
2. Lakshminarayana S. and Prakasam P., Decentralised Planning in Andhra Pradesh - Problems and Constraints, Eighth Plan Perspectives of Andhra Pradesh, Feb. 2-3, 1989, Centre for Economic and Social Studies, Hyderabad, pp. 6-7.
3. Rao, B, Surya, Decentralised planning. Experience in Andhra Pradesh, Eighth plan perspectives of Andhra Pradesh, Feb. 2-3, 1989, CESS, Hyderabad.
4. Barua, Bhaskar, Status paper on Decentralised Planning in Assam, National seminar on Decentralised Planning, Feb. 13-14, 1988, State Planning Institute, Lucknow, p. 5.
5. Barua Bhaskar, op. cit., pp.5-6.
6. Govt. of Bihar, Planning Department, Draft Annual Plan 1988-89, p. x-xi.
7. Giridhar, C.B., Decentralised Planning, Experience and Lessons of Gujarat, National seminar on Decentralised planning, State Planning Institute, Lucknow, Feb. 13-14, 1988, p. 4.
8. Government of Himachal Pradesh, Draft Annual Plan, 1987-88, Planning Department, Shimla, p. 31.
9. Govt. of Himachal Pradesh, op. cit., p. 32.
10. Kumar, Ajit, Decentralised Planning in Jammu and Kashmir (Status paper), National Seminar on Decentralised Planning, February 13-14, 1988, State Planning Institute, Lucknow, p. 1.
11. Mathew George, Karnataka Model of Decentralisation, All India seminar on issues in decentralised planning in India, May 14-16, 1987, Instt. of Management in Govt., Trivandrum, p. 5.
12. Govt. of Kerala, Formulation of Eighth Five Year Plan (1990-95), Background paper on Decentralised planning, State Planning Board, Trivandrum, p. 6.
13. Ibid., p. 7.
14. Govt. of Kerala - op. cit., p. 8.
15. Rajan, M.P., Status paper on Decentralised Planning process in Madhya Pradesh, National seminar on Decentralised Planning, 13-14, Feb. 1988, State Planning Institute, Lucknow, p. 1.

16. Government of Orissa, Guidelines for the subject matter Working group for district level planning, Hand book of circulars on District Planning, Planning and Coordination Deptt., p. 1.

17. Garg, S.P., District Planning Rajasthan, National Seminar on Decentralised planning, Feb. 13-14, 1988, State Planning Institute, Lucknow, p. 1.

18. Garg, S.P. op. cit., p. 3.

19. Sarkar, Bikram, Status paper on Decentralised planning, West Bengal, National seminar on Decentralised planning, Feb. 13-14, 1988, State Planning Institute, Lucknow, p. 1.

III

Functional Decentralisation

For operationalisation of micro planning, identification of schemes and activities to be planned and implemented at the district level and below is very crucial. This necessitates to defining the scope of the micro level plan explicitly to make it clear to the planning and implementing agencies their real roles leaving no scope for confusion and duplication in their role performance. Moreover, the quantum of fund to be earmarked for plan implementation at district level and below have also to be decided on the basis of the schemes to be taken up at these levels.

As is the case of institutional infrastructure for micro planning, the pattern adopted for functional decentralisation also differs from state to state. Inspite of this diversity, with a few exception, the schemes in most of the states have been categorised as state and district sector schemes. The basic principle followed in the identification of the district sector schemes is that the scheme's benefits would be confined to the district. Similarly the schemes which benefit more than one district, irrespective of their location are categorised as state sector schemes. Thus schemes like major and medium irrigation, major industries, state highways, power generation, university education are outside the purview of micro level planning and fall under the category of state sector scheme. Similarly, schemes like agricultural production and minor irrigation, soil conservation, animal husbandry, forestry, village and small industries, warehousing and marketing, etc. are of relevance to individual districts and hence are classified under district sector schemes. In the following paragraphs a review has been made on the functional decentralisation of schemes in different states.

ANDHRA PRADESH

In the state of Andhra Pradesh as stated earlier besides the state the district as well as mandals are also adopted as units for planning and development. Therefore, concomitant with this, plan schemes are also divided into state, district and mandal sector schemes. This is a recent development and in due course after gaining experience in this field the list of district and mandal level schemes might be modified. But, for the time being sectors like agriculture and allied activities, rural development, minor irrigation, rural electrification, social services have been categorised as district level schemes (Table 3.1) whereas community development, irrigation, wells, animal husbandry and fisheries, health and rural sanitation, education, communication, cooperation, cottage industries, women welfare, social welfare, emergency relief, self help programme etc. are classified as mandal praja parishad schemes (Table 3.2).[1]

ASSAM

The State of Assam is unique so far as the functional decentralisation for micro planning is concerned. It has sub-divisional level schemes and state level schemes.[2] Thus the schemes concerned with the lives of common people, particularly in the sectors of Agriculture, Veterinary, Fisheries, Cooperation, Irrigation, Cottage Industry, Health and Family Welfare, Primary Education, Adult Education, Social Forestry, Village Roads etc. are generally planned at the sub-division level. Other schemes which are highly technical in nature requiring huge investment and constant supervision and guidance from experts and senior officers of the Headquarters are treated as state level schemes. Thus projects and programmes relating to generation of power, major and medium irrigation, major and medium industries, university education, professional and technical institutions, research and training programmes, state highways, inland water transport etc. are treated as state level schemes. It has been decided by the state government to cover 22 sectors initially in the sub-divisional plan. In due course, more sectors will be added to this list.

Table 3.1
District Sector Schemes in Andhra Pradesh

I.	**Agriculture and Allied Services**
	Crop Husbandry
	Soil and Water Conservation
	Animal Husbandry
	Dairy Development
	Fisheries
	Marketing
II.	**Rural Development**
	I.R.D.P.
	D.P.A.P.
	N.R.E.P.
	R.L.E.G.P.
III.	**Irrigation & Flood Control**
	Minor Irrigation
IV.	**Energy**
	Rural Electrification
V.	**Industry & Minerals**
	Village and Small Industries
	Large and Medium
VI.	**Transport**
	Mini Ports and Light Houses
	Roads & Bridges
	Traffic Control
VII.	**General Economic Services**
	Economic Advice and Statistics
	Tourism
VIII.	**Social Services**
	General Education
	Sports and Youth Services
	Technical Education
	Art & Culture
	Medical and Public Health
	Water Supply and Sanitation
	Housing
	Urban Development

(Contd.)

Welfare of Scheduled Tribe and Backward Classes
Labour and Employment
Social Security and welfare

IX. **General Services**
Stationery and Printing
Chief Engineer Buildings
Mandal Buildings

Table 3.2
Mandal Sector Schemes in A.P.

Mandal Praja Parishad Level Scheme

1. Community Development
2. Irrigation wells
3. Animal husbandry and fisheries
4. Health and Rural sanitation
5. Education
6. Social education
7. Communication
8. Cooperation
9. Cottage industries
10. Women welfare
11. Social welfare
12. Emergency relief
13. Collection of statistics
14. Self help programme and
15. Trusts.

BIHAR

The development schemes in this state have been classified in two categories viz., state sector and district sector schemes. Schemes pertaining to the sectors like major irrigation (suwarnarekha project), major industries, national highways, university education, agricultural research and education, Chota Nagpur autonomous development authority, flood control are some of the state sector schemes, whereas, district sector schemes consist of sectors of local importance such as crop husbandry, fisheries, animal husbandry, rural development programmes, small scale industries, water supply, primary education, forestry, minor irrigation etc.[3] The specific schemes pertaining to these sectors to be planned and executed can be seen from Table 3.3.

GUJARAT

This state has adopted a different pattern for classifying schemes under micro level planning. These classifications are based on the type of fund available for taking up the schemes at the district level and below. There are discretionary funds and incentive outlay. The district level schemes as well as those planned and implemented below the district level have also been categorised accordingly as (a) schemes admissible under discretionary outlays, (b) schemes admissible under incentive outlay, and (c) schemes not admissible under discretionary and incentive outlays.

Table 3.3
District Sector Schemes—Bihar

Crop Husbandry	1. Plant protection
	2. Commercial crops
	3. Agricultural Engineering
	4. Horticulture and Tobacco Development
	5. Manures and fertilisers
	6. Extension of farmers training
	7. Dryland farmers training
	8. Dairy development.
Sugarcane Development	1. Subsidy on seed transplantation
	2. Subsidy on seed production
	3. Sugarcane demonstration
	4. Subsidy on pesticides
	5. Subsidy on urea spraying
	6. Subsidy on moist hot air treatment
	7. Subsidy on spraying equipments
	8. Subsidy on bullock drawn cane carts.

(Contd.)

Agrl. Marketing	1. Construction of market yards
	2. Development of hats/mandies.
Spl. Programme for RD	1. IRDP
	2. NREP
	3. DPAP
	4. DWCRA
Land Reforms	1. Financial assistance to allottees of surplus land
	2. Consolidation of holdings.
Sewerage and Water Supply	1. Sewerage and drainage
	2. Conversion of service latrines into watershed latrines
	3. Piped water supply
	4. Drinking water wells
	5. Hand operated tube wells
	6. Drilled tube wells
	7. Rural sanitation
Urban Development	1. Rickshaw puller welfare scheme
	2. Environment improvement of urban slums
Labour and Labour Welfare	1. Rehabilitation of bonded labour
	2. Establishment of rural labour welfare centres
	3. Organisation of rural camps.
Welfare of Backward Classes	1. Pre-matric scholarships for children of those engaged in unclean occupations.
	2. Book bank for medical & engg. students.
	3. Stipends
	4. Hostel grants to girl students in schools
	5. Supply of girl students in school.
Construction of Girls Hostel	1. Opening, maintenance and construction of residential schools & hostels.
Social Welfare	1. Welfare of handicapped women and child welfare, beggers home.
Nutrition	1. S.N.P.
Dist. Planning	1. District planning.

Panchayat	1. Matching incentive grants to Gram Panchayat
	2. Grants to Z.P.
	3. Grants for construction of Z.P. Bhavan
	4. Grants to ZP for construction
Special Area Development	1. Schemes for special areas under RDD
	2. Schemes for Kolhan areas under welfare department.
Cooperation	1. Cooperative credit
	2. Share capital to urban cooperative banks
Non-conventional Sources of Energy	1. Demonstration of improved chullah.
	2. NPBD.
Village and Small Industries	1. Handicrafts
	2. Handloom
	3. Sericulture
Roads and Bridges	1. Major and minor district roads.
	2. Rural and urban roads
	3. Roads in sugar cane areas
Tourism and Pilgrim Development	1. Construction of tourist and pilgrim centres
General Education	1. Non-formal education
	2. Elementary education
	3. Secondary education
Sports & Youth Services	1. Construction of stadium
Physical Education	1. Development of playground.
Art and Culture	1. Grants to district/sub-divisional/private libraries.
Health	1. Minor works for PHC, Addl. PHC, SHC and referral hospitals.
Minor Irrigation	1. Private tubewells
	2. Irrigation dug wells
	3. Water tanks
	4. Lift irrigation schemes of the Deptt.
	5. Tubewell projects (World Bank assisted)

(Contd.)

Soil & Water Conservation	1. S & WC in rainfed areas and in catchment of irrigation project dams.
Animal Husbandry	1. Veterinary and Health services
	2. Schemes for creating offices for newly created Deoghar district
	3. Construction of building for class I veterinary dispensaries under SCP.
	4. Strengthening of hospitals and dispensaries.
	5. Cattle, poultry, sheep and goat, piggery development.
	6. Fodder development.
Dairy Development	1. Milk chilling
	2. Rural dairy development
	3. Reclamation and development of tank fisheries
	4. Development of reservoir fisheries.
Forest and Environment Development	1. Social forestry
	2. Rural fuel wood plantation
	3. Urban forestry and roadside plantation.
Community Development	1. Construction of block building
	2. Small schemes on recommendations of MPs and MLAs.

It can be seen from the given statement that the schemes pertaining to Minimum Needs Programme like Rural Electrification, Rural Roads, Primary Education, Adult Education, Primary Health facility, Water supply, Rural housing, Nutrition and Environmental improvement of slums have been included under the category 'discretionary outlays'. Other than these, schemes related to Agriculture Development, Minor Irrigation, Soil Conservation, Animal Husbandry, Local Development Works, Rural and small industries, Tourism, Technical Education, Labour and Labour welfare, welfare and backward classes, Family Welfare also form part of this category of schemes. Whereas, schemes admissible under incentive outlays are mostly construction work for primary education or primary health centre, Animal husbandry, Dairy development, Community development and panchayats, local development works, rural and small industries, general education, technical education and welfare of backward classes (Table 3.4). Only major schemes related to all the aspects to be covered under the first two categories of schemes have been placed under the third category and which covers schemes not admissible under discretionary and incentive outlays, which are planned and executed by the sectoral departments utilising normal allocation.

KARNATAKA

As in the case of A.P. the Karnataka government has also effected functional decentralisation at district and mandal levels. Three levels of schemes have been identified namely—state sector, zilla parishad sector and mandal panchayat sector on the basis of their location and extent of benefits. Like in other states, the state sector schemes in Karnataka also include major projects pertaining to irrigation, power, industries, education, transport. The Z.P. sector consists of 20 schemes pertaining to agriculture and allied sectors, health and education, rural development programmes etc. (Table 3.5) whereas, the mandal panchayat schemes include sanitation and health, forests, marketing, drinking water supply, land reforms, roads, regulation of grazing land and street lighting in villages.

MADHYA PRADESH

The State of Madhya Pradesh has also prepared list of schemes which will be taken up for planning and implementation by the Janpad Panchayats at the block level[4], schemes suggested for block level planning consists of Agriculture, Forestry, Veterinary and Animal Husbandry, Health and Family Planning, Public Works, Public Health and Engineering, Education, Social Welfare, and Cooperation. (Table 3.6)

MAHARASHTRA

In the state of Maharashtra also there are only two broad categories of the schemes namely state level and district level schemes. The schemes which need to be planned at the local level for optimum exploitation of the natural and other resources of the district have been identified as district level schemes. However, the experience of this state has shown that all the schemes listed out as district level schemes are not planned at the district level and some of these schemes are planned at the state level. This situation arises in certain specific cases (1) when new plan schemes are introduced; (2) when centrally sponsored schemes are adopted on sharing basis; (3) when schemes for local benefits require funds larger

Table 3.4
Illustrative list of schemes admissible and not admissible under Decentralised District Planning, in the State of Gujarat.

Sectors/ Sub-Sector of development	*Schemes admissible under discretionary and incentive outlays*
1	2
(A) Minimum Needs Programme:	
1. Rural Electrification	1. Electrification for all purposes in respect of the villages already electrified for agricultural purposes. 2. New works of rural electrification 3. Street lights in villages 4. Street lights in Harijanvas, Halpativas and free plots. 5. Providing electric connections upto 1.5 point (within maximum limit of Rs. 300) in the houses of the weaker sections of the Society/ Harijans who are residing in free plot area.
2. Rural Roads	1. Rural Approach Roads (villages not having any basic facilities) 2. Approach roads in which earth work has been done under programmes for scarcity, NREP etc. 3. Approach roads remaining to be taken up under Taluka 20 year plan 4. Roads plyable by ST buses all the year round (preference should be given to villages which have not received any benefit under decentralised District Planning during the last 3 years).

Schemes admissible only under incentive outlay	*Schemes not admissible under discretionary and incentive outlays*
3	4
	1. Schemes of providing House connections on individual basis.
	1. State Highways, Major District Roads, other District Roads. 2. Land Acquisition works 3. Major Bridges 4. Roads in Urban & Cantonment Areas 5. Repairing of Major Roads damaged in natural calamities. 6. Roads coming under NREP, Rural Employment Guarantee Scheme, Scarcity or Budgetted roads. 7. Machinery such as Road Rollers, Bull dozers etc.

(Contd.)

1	2
	5. Small works of missing links viz., culverts, small bridges, deep cause ways and other cross drainage works (without which existing roads cannot be utilised). 6. Roads connecting 2 villages (preference should be given to villages which are not connected with any other villages). 7. Improvement of Existing Roads (only in cases where there is a danger to life or hazard to traffic). 8. Road works in Harijanwas/Free plot areas (only if a minimum of 25 to 30 families are residing there).
3. Primary Education	1. New class rooms for primary schools (in villages in which not a single room is existing). 2. Additional rooms in primary schools (schools in which more than one class is accommodated in one room and in villages where class rooms are required as per the prevailing norms of the Department of Education) 3. Additional rooms in primary schools (in villages which do not receive any other facility under Minimum Needs) 4. Incomplete school rooms (in cases where Departmental/Legal inquiry is not in progress). 5. Necessary facilities in Primary schools - such as Hand Pumps, urinals lavatories, electrification etc.

3	4
1. Buildings for Balmandirs 2. Buildings for Balwadis. 3. Compound wall.	1. Furniture, Laboratory Equipment 2. Library, books, uniforms, sports equipment 3. Staff Quarters 4. Unnecessary repairing works such as white wash, painting etc.

(Contd.)

1	2
	6. Repairing works of primary school rooms (where there is a danger to the safety and health of the students). 7. Additional rooms in girls' schools. 8. Class rooms for "Buniyadi" (Basic) shala & Ashram shalas. 9. Construction of store room and kitchens for Mid-day-Meal programme (within the maximum limit of Rs. 25000).
4. Adult Education	This being Centrally sponsored and individual oriented scheme, no scheme can be taken up under this head.
5. Primary Health	1. Buildings for Primary Health Centres/sub-centres. 2. Works of Capital Expenditure 3. Operation Theatres 4. Childrens' Ward 5. Burns ward 6. MaternityHospitals 7. Facilities for Drinking water and Electrification 8. Surgical instruments: Refrigerator, Leproscopic Machine, X-Ray Machine 9. Compound wall 10. Govt. Ayurvedic Dispensaries (construction & major extn. work)
6. Water Supply	1. New Water Supply Works in problem villages

3	4
1. Ambulance 2. Mortuary Van 3. Mobile Dispensaries 4. Eye camps 5. Camps for Diognosis & treatment (Preference should be given to T.B., Leprosy & blindness. Ayurvedic, Allopathic, Homeo-pathic). 6. Air conditioning of burns ward in Hospital. 7. Air conditioning of operation theatres 8. Mobile Ayurvedic Dispensaries 9. Schemes of Capital nature for extension of rooms or buildings only (Preference should be given to T.B. and removal of blindness).	1. Doctors' Quarters 2. Staff quarters 3. Intercom, store room or kitchen in hospital. 4. Purchase of medicines 5. Assistance to patients for any kind of disease. 6. Facilities in Govt. District Pan-chayat/Nagar Panchayat Dispen-saries/Hospitals (e.g. water cooler, furniture etc.) 7. T.B. Senatorium 8. Assistance to disabled for equip-ment 9. Equipments such as mattresses, cots and blankets.
	1. Scheme of providing water connections on individual basis.

(Contd.)

1	2
	2. New Water Supply Works in Non-Problem villages 3. Tank, Stand Post: Pipeline, standpost in Harijanwas. 4. New Water Supply works in new 'free plot' areas. 5. Activising closed No source Schemes (in cases where legal, departmental enquiry is not in progress). 6. Water Supply Stations, Wells and Boring works. 7. Water Supply repair works in cases where funds are not forthcoming from other sources and the scheme has had to be closed as a result.
7. Rural Housing	1. As the approach of Decentralised Planning is against taking up individual beneficiary oriented schemes, no scheme can be taken up under this head.
8. Nutrition	1. New buildings for Nutrition centres (within a maximum limit of Rs. 25000). 2. Major repair works of Nutrition centres. 3. Equipments for Nutrition Centres such as for preparing food (where not available) and equipments such as plates, spoons etc. which render more convenience to the children for breakfast (within a maximum limit of Rs. 2000).
9. Environmental improvement of slums	1. Works relating to Minimum Needs as specified above such as primary education, drinking water, street light etc.

3	4
	2. Maintenance expenditure of water supply schemes. 3. Water tanker.
	1. Assistance on individual. 2. Assistance for construction of buildings on individual basis.
	1. Assistance to Nutrition Centres for furniture, codiments & spices.

(Contd.)

1	2
B. Programmes other than Minimum Needs Programme	
1. Agriculture Development	1. No schemes can be taken as family-oriented and individual-oriented schemes are being implemented by Agriculture Dept. and under the Integrated Rural Dev. Programme.
2. Minor Irrigation	1. Construction of check Dams. 2. Construction of tube-wells (which can also be used for providing drinking water). 3. Construction of New tanks. 4. Repair of percolation Tanks 5. Improvement of canals
3. Soil Conservation	1. Construction of flood protection walls
4. Animal Husbandry	1. Construction of Cattle Dispensary 2. Repair of Cattle dispensary buildings 3. Travis
5. Dairy Development	
6. Community Development & Panchayats	

3	4
	1. Education-oriented tours 2. Individual assistance schemes such as seeds, fertilizers, Agricultural implements, any type of pump, gypsum treatment etc.
	1. Purchase of rigs for boring wells. 2. Digging or repair of wells on an individual basis. 3. Pipe lines in individual farms.
1. Cattle Pen 2. Animal disease Diagnosis	1. Ram Depot 2. Providing medicines in Cattle dispensaries 3. Cattle exhibition/show, Administrative office or staff quarters etc.
1. Construction of Buildings for Milk producer's societies-Maximum cost of building limited to Rs. 100,000 (within limit of Rs. 75000 of decentralised district planning grant for backward talukas and for other areas Rs. 50000).	1. Schemes to give transport cost of milk producers societies.
1. Panchayat Ghar	1. Any sort of facilities for Panchayat Ghar.

(Contd.)

1	2
7. Local Development Works	1. Public Lavatories 2. Public Urinals 3. Cemented Cattle Paths.
8. Rural & Small Industries	1. Schemes of capital expenditure of equipments for training centres run by Panchayats or Government.
9. Tourism	1. Provision of Drinking water facilities in Tourism Centres.
10. General Eaucation	
11. Technical Education	1. Construction of additional rooms in ITI.s. 2. Provision of Equipment in ITIs (Capital nature)
12. Labour & Labour Welfare	1. Buildings for Rural Labour Welfare Centres.
13. Welfare of Backward Classes	

3	4
1. Cremation Sheds 2. Washing ghats 3. Fire Fighter 4. Stone-Paving works	1. S.T. Pickup stands 2. Marketing yards or Vegetable yards.
1. Hostel for trainees 2. Construction of additional rooms in craftsmen training centres.	1. Staff Quarters 2. Assistance to individual craftsmen for training.
	1. Provision of Luxury bus, Auditorium or any other type of facility.
1. Buildings for High Schools. 2. Compound wall for High Schools. 3. Major repair of High school buildings. 4. Additional rooms in girls' schools. 5. Provision of facilities for drinking water, lavatories urinals or electrification in High schools. 6. Major repairs of classroom in post-basic schools/ashram schools and provision of auxiliary basic facilities such as drinking water.	1. Staff Quarters 2. Equipments involving recurring expenditure (e.g. chalk, black board furniture, books, etc.)
1. Building for Polytechnic	1. Staff Quarters 2. Administrative Office Buildings.
1. Hostel for women belonging to ST/SC.	

(Contd.)

1	2
14. Family Welfare	1. Incentive for family planning Operation (Rs. 50 per person and according to constructions of GAD Circulars No. JAP-1081-3982-Y dated 29.3.84.
15. Miscellaneous	1. Construction District Planning office (if setting in rented building) 2. Publishing reports pertaining to Decentralised District Planning. 3. To conduct survey/studies sanctioned by State Govt. 4. To purchase books for library of District Planning Board (except News Papers & Magazines within yearly limit of Rs. 3000) 5. Machinery for Statistical work (with the prior sanction of State Govt.) 6. Garage for jeep of District Planning Officer (for districts where no such facility exists).

than would be provided within the district allocations. In this state also both at the district as well as at state level the sectors to be planned are common (Table 3.7).

ORISSA

The state of Orissa, has also classified the plan schemes in the normal way as state sector and district sector schemes. As large projects and programmes require a state level decision and high technical expertise, these have been included in the state list. In addition to this the projects covering more than one district or benefitting more than one district or even the state as a whole are also included in the state sector schemes. It can be seen from the statement (Table 3.8) that Professional Education and Research Institutes along with Major and Medium Projects belonging to Flood Control, Industries, Generation and Distribution of Power, Agricultural Development,

3	4
	1. Construction of Garage 2. Gobar Gas Plant 3. Scout guide activity, sports equipments, water sports complex, Radio, Television. 4. Uniforms for Home Guard and Border Security Force.

National and State Highways, Major District Roads, Sub-Health Centres and District and Sub-division Hospitals etc. are state sector schemes. The remaining schemes, projects and programmes which are of local importance either from the viewpoint of proper utilisation of available physical resources, meeting local needs, filling in some gaps in the sectoral programmes and development of some local infrastructure etc. have been classified as district sector schemes. The illustrated list of the district sector schemes is shown in the Table 3.8.

UTTAR PRADESH

Under the decentralised planning process in this state various planned schemes have been classified into two categories namely state sector, and district sector schemes as in other states.[5] The basis of this classification is mainly location and coverage of the schemes. In this state the sectors for development for state as well as district sector schemes are common and they differ from each other only in the type/magnitude of the schemes. Thus agriculture, horticulture, land reforms, irrigation, land and water conservation, storage and warehousing, animal husbandry, fisheries, forestry, panchayati raj, community development, cooperation, electricity, industries, roads and transportation, education, health and medical care and labour welfare are the major sectors which are planned and implemented at both the state as well as district level. The details of the state as well as district sector schemes can be seen from the Table 3.9. However, the Government of Uttar Pradesh, has plans to re-classify the state and district sector schemes and detailed exercise for arriving at this list in a more rational way is in the process.

Table 3.5
Zilla Parishad Level Schemes - Karnataka

1. Agriculture
2. Animal husbandry
3. Welfare of Scheduled Castes and Scheduled Tribes and backward classes.
4. District roads and bridges
5. Administrative and other buildings
6. Public health
7. Irrigation
8. Cottage industry
9. Horticulture
10. Cooperation
11. Education and social education
12. Fisheries
13. Provision for essential commodities
14. Rural electrification
15. I.R.D.P.
16. N.R.E.P.
17. D.P.A.P.
18. R.L.E.G.P.
19. Trysem
20. Antyodaya have also been transferred to the Zilla Parishad.

Table 3.6

Janapad Panchayat Level (Block) Schemes —M.P.

Agriculture

(a) Kharif and Rabi programme
(b) requirement of seed for kharif and rabi season
(c) scrutiny of adjustment of loan and its repayment in the accounts of cultivators
(d) recommendation - selection of beneficiaries for beneficiary oriented schemes.

Forest

(a) approval of nistari schemes
(b) approval of alternate arrangements for fodder supply in areas of national parks or Abhayaranyas
(c) implementation of social forestry programme and distribution of bamboos/timber logs and nistari fuel.

Veterinary and Animal Husbandry

(a) cattle development programme
(b) disease control and its organisation

Health and Family Planning

(a) Supervision of Primary Health Centre, Mini PHC, Addl. Primary Health Centre, Subsidiary Health Centres, Sub-Health Centres, Civil Dispensaries, Ayurvedic, Yunani and Homeopathic Hospitals.
(b) Supervision of the implementation of Family welfare programme.
(c) National programme of Eradication of blindness, National T.B. Control and National Health programme.

Public Works

Supervision of rural road construction programme under MNP and maintenance of village roads.

Public Health Engineering

(a) Fixation of areal priority for taking up works for the supply of drinking water to problem villages.
(b) Determination of H.Q. of mechanics for maintenance and repairs of handpumps in rural areas.

Education

(a) Supervision and inspection of primary and middle school institutions.
(b) Development of education within the jurisdiction.
(c) Framing outlines for implementing compulsory education programme for persons of 6-14 age group.

(Contd.)

Social Welfare

(a) Scrutiny and recommendation of cases for social security pension.
(b) Discrimination of areas for opening of classes for adult education.
(c) Disbursement of honorarium to instructors engaged for adult education classes.
(d) Supervision and control of the work of social education organisers.
(e) Supervision of institutions run by social welfare department in Janapad areas.
(f) Grant-in-aid to institutions engaged in women and child welfare on the recommendation of Janapad panchayats.
(g) Supervision of activities related to rural nutrition programme, rural balwadis etc.

Cooperation

Investigation of factitious loans given by cooperative societies.

Table 3.7
District Level Schemes—Maharashtra State

Agriculture & Allied Services

1. Creation of irrigation facilities for Taluka seed farm.
2. Purchase of plant protection equipment.
3. Plant protection subsidy for pesticides, raticides etc.
4. Opening of retail outlets for stocking of fertilizers.
5. Intensive programme for oilseed production.
6. Subsidy for improved farm implements.
7. Intensive production of pulses crop.
8. Subsidy for inputs.
9. Supply of bullocks and bullock carts to Tribals.
10. Special Component Plan for Scheduled Castes and Neo-Budhists - grant of financial assistance.
11. Divisional and district horticultural offices.
12. Strengthening of nurseries.
13. Renovation of country mango and ber trees.
14. Capital subsidy for horticulture development for small and marginal farmers for oranges, musambies, kagdilime and guava.
15. Development of cocoa and coffee.
16. Financial assistance to allottees of surplus land.
17. Financial assistance to Tribals for restoration of alienated lands.
18. Financial assistance to Tribal tenant purchasers to pay off purchase price under tenancy laws.

19. Minor irrigation schemes.
20. Minor irrigation (state sector).
21. Bunding and terracing programme.
22. Plantation and afforestation.
23. Ayacut development.
24. Strengthening of the offices of District Animal Husbandry officers.
25. Training to farmers.
26. Stipend for training of livestock supervisor.
27. Establishment and construction of buildings for veterinary polyclinics.
28. Providing of medicine to existing veterinary institutions.
29. Establishment and construction of buildings for veterinary dispensaries/ veterinary aid centres.
30. Upgradation of veterinary aid centres.
31. Establishment of mobile epizootic control unit/veterinary clinics.
32. Subsidy for vaccine to control foot and mouth diseases.
33. Establishment of key village centres.
34. Supply of cross-bred bulls, under premium bull scheme.
35. Establishment of district level project cell.
36. Rearing of cross-bred heifers.
37. Poultry programme.
38. Distribution of cockerels.
39. Construction of residential and non-residential buildings at intensive poultry dev. block.
40. Distribution of chicks to beneficiaries.
41. Organisation of fodder demonstration plots.
42. Publicity and mass propaganda.
43. District set up under Dairy development Department.
44. Strengthening of cooperative district set up.
45. Managerial subsidy.
46. Capital grants to cooperatives for purchase of milk cans, testing equipments etc.
47. Incentive to small dairy cooperative societies for continuing individual testing during lean season.
48. Training to secretaries of dairy cooperatives.
49. Training programme specially designed for Adivasi and Scheduled Caste farmers and other weaker sections.
50. Supply of dry pregnant buffaloes.
51. Fodder cultivation.

(Contd.)

52. Extension of calf rearing unit of Daptchary, Aarey, Palgarh and increasing the govt. herd for supply of cross-bred heifers.
53. Government milk schemes.
54. Establishment of fish seed production farms.
55. Development of fisheries in brackish water.
56. Training of fisher youths.
57. Fish farming in impounded water.
58. Preservation, transport and marketing of fish.
59. Mechanisation of fishing crafts on improvement of fishing boats.
60. Assistance for supply of fishery requisite.
61. Grant of loan to fishermen.
62. Development of fishery cooperatives.
63. Improvement of fishing harbours.
64. Grant of subsidy to fishermen towards payment of insurance premium.
65. Establishment of central nurseries.
66. Community School nurseries.
67. Plantation of forest species for local and commercial uses.
68. Reforestation of degraded forests.
69. Afforestation of denuded forests through poor and unemployed persons.
70. Wild life and nature conservation.
71. Protection of forests.
72. Establishment of firewood and timber depot.
73. Development of minor forests produce.
74. Development of fodder resources.
75. Construction of sheds for labour and field staff.
76. Tusser cultivation.
77. Supply of bullock carts to Adivasis and forest labourers.
78. Felling of trees from malki lands of Scheduled Tribes.
79. Plantation of fruit trees on lands belonging to Scheduled Castes and Scheduled Tribes.
80. Rural fuelwood plantation.
81. A tree for a child.
82. Establishment of central nurseries.
83. Raising of plantation on road-side and canal-side.
84. Maharashtra social forest project plantation.

Table 3.8
State and District Sector Schemes—Orissa

State Sector Schemes	*District Sector Schemes*
1. **Agriculture and Allied Services**	1. **Agriculture and Allied Services**
(i) Research and Education	(i) Crop husbandry
(ii) Headquarters programme	(ii) Soil and water conservation
(iii) Territorial plantations under Forestry	(iii) Social farm forestry
(iv) Forest research	(iv) Fisheries
(v) Central Dairying	(v) Animal husbandry
(vi) Fisheries research	(vi) Dairy development food storage and warehousing corporation
	(vii) Agriculture marketing.
2. **Rural Development**	2. **Rural Development**
(i) Education and training	(i) Integrated Rural Dev. programme
(ii) Headquarters programmes	(ii) Economic Rehabilitation of rural poor
	(iii) Drought Prone area programme
	(iv) National Rural Employment programme
	(v) Rural landless employment guarantee programme
	(vi) Community development
	(vii) Panchayats
	(viii) Special area programme
	(ix) Land Reforms
3. **Irrigation and Flood Control**	3. **Irrigation and Flood Control**
(i) Major and medium projects	(i) Minor irrigation (flow)
(ii) Investigation and research	(ii) Lift irrigation
(iii) Major flood control	(iii) Dug wells
	(iv) Flood control programmes
	(v) Command Area Development.

(Contd.)

State Sector Schemes	*District Sector Schemes*
4. **Power**	4. **Power**
(i) Generation and distribution of power	(i) Non-conventional sources of energy including bio-gas.
	(ii) Rural electrification programmes and energisation of pumpsets
5. **Industries and Minerals**	5. **Industries and Minerals**
(i) Large and Medium Industries	(i) Small scale and village industries
(ii) Mineral development	(ii) Artisan - based industries and handicrafts
	(iii) Handloom and sericulture etc.
6. **Transport**	6. **Transport**
(i) Ports and light houses	(i) Other district roads
(ii) Shipping	(ii) Panchayat and Gram panchayat roads
(iii) Civil aviation	(iii) Rural roads
(iv) National and state highways	(iv) Road transport
(v) Major District Roads	(v) Inland water transport (within the district)
7. **Science, Technology and Environment**	7. **Science, Technology and Environment**
(i) Scientific Research (including science and technology)	(i) Ecology and environment water pollution control
8. **Education, Sports and Culture**	8. **Education**
(i) University Education Professional and Technical education	(i) Elementary and primary education
(ii) Research and training	(ii) Adult education
(iii) Secondary education	
(iv) Sports, culture and youth services.	

(Contd.)

State Sector Schemes	District Sector Schemes
9. Medical and Public Health	**9. Medical and Public Health**
(i) District and sub-division Hospitals	(i) Primary Health Centre
(ii) Special Health Centres	(ii) Dispensaries (all types)
(iii) Research and training	(iii) Medical and Dhai centres
	(iv) Village Health guides etc.
10. Water Supply Housing and Urban Development	**10. Water Supply Housing and Urban Development**
(i) Police Housing state capital projects	(i) Rural water supply
(ii) Others	(ii) Sanitation
	(iii) Rural Housing
	(iv) Urban development
11. Labour and Labour Welfare	**11. Labour and Labour Welfare**
(i) Welfare training, employment exchanges, special employment schemes	(i) Rural labour welfare
	(ii) Rural employment
12. Social Welfare and Nutrition	**12. Social Welfare and Nutrition**
	(i) Social welfare
	(ii) Nutrition
13. General services including jails, stationery and printing, public works and etc.	13. NIL

Table 3.9
State and District Sector Schemes—Uttar Pradesh

State Sector	*District Sector*
Agriculture Sector	
1. Establishment of seed standardisation institute	1. Plan for multiplication and storage of HYV seeds
2. Set-up of fertiliser and pesticides quality control laboratory	2. Plan for center sponsored intensive oilseed development programme
3. Establishment of Central Soil control and testing laboratory	3. Plan for Dry land agriculture
4. Plan for organisation of training camps with regard to set-up Janata bio-gas plants.	4. Plan for strengthening plant protection services in plan area.
5. Plan for strengthening the quality control lab for chemical pesticides	
6. Set-up of seed multiplication farms in the area of 200 acres and alone	
7. Organization of farm exhibitions and Kissan Melas.	
8. Plan for strengthening Agriculture extension and poultry	
9. Plan for extension, exhibition and distribution of modern agricultural implements.	
10. Plan for programme Agricultural statistics in U.P.	
11. Plan for providing economic assistance for agricultural activities to surrendered dacoits and victimised farmers	
12. Establishment of Monitoring Cell with regard to the recommendation on National Commission on Agriculture.	
13. Policy to provide training to unemployed persons with technical background under Agro services Center schemes.	

(Contd.)

State Sector	*District Sector*
Horticulture Sector	
1. State plan for agriculture 2. State plan for strengthening and extension of State Institute of Fruit protection and packaging.	1. Establishment and strengthening of industrial production and seed standardisation units. 2. Betal leaves development programme.
Sugarcane Development	
1. Plan for Pest control through areal and ground spray methods	1. Plan for providing crop production equipment on scheduled rates. 2. Plan for intensive fertiliser development programme.
Agricultural Marketing	
	1. Plan for providing subsidy to regulated markets for land and infrastructure development.
Animal Husbandry	
1. Education on Animal Husbandry and training. 2. Cattle health and medical services 3. Research and statistics of animal husbandry 4. Poultry development 5. Sheep and wool development 6. Fodder development 7. Piggery development.	1. Strengthening of veterinary dispensaries and setting up of Mobile veterinary units and A.I. Centres. 2. Setting up of Intensive Poultry Development programme and promotion of poultry development project. 3. Extension and strengthening of Health services for sheep and goats. 4. Programme for strengthening and extension of wool analyses, grading and marketing centres. 5. Plan for development of fodder seeds 6. Plan for purchase and distribution of exotic breds.

(Contd.)

State Sector	District Sector
Fisheries	
1. Training and education in fisheries 2. Investment of share capital in fisheries development corporation for the programme of construction of large ponds.	1. Development of fresh water fish
Forest Development	
1. Afforestation of the species having economic and industrial importance. 2. Training of forest personnel 3. Intensive management for wild-life sanctuaries. 4. Survey and development of minor forest produce.	1. Programme for social forestry in urban areas. 2. Afforestation of species for fire-wood production.
Land Reforms	
1. Consolidation of holdings. 2. Special survey for the impact of land reforms.	1. Plan for land distribution through surplus land procurement 2. Financial assistance to the land distributors of Gram Sabha.
Ground Water Survey	
1. Plan for identifying new water sources and development of advanced technology	
Minor Irrigation Private	
1. Plan for new plants and equipments.	1. Development of Bore-wells
Minor Irrigation	
1. State bore-well plan aidded by World Bank	1. Construction of low cost channels below Rs. 50,000

(Contd.)

State Sector	*District Sector*
Land & Water Conservation	
1. Integrated Agriculture Plan for the development of fallows. 2. Plan for rennovating soil conservation programmes in plains. 3. Plan for strengthening training centres for soil conservation in plains. 4. Development of remote Survey Technology through satellites.	1. Plan for alkaline land development 2. Plan for soil and water conservation in plains. 3. Plan for soil conservation and community lands in plain areas.
Storage and Ware Housing	
1. Construction of godowns.	
Village and Small Industries	
1. Industrial cooperation 2. Marketing through small industries cooperation 3. Monitoring and evaluation 4. Assistance for small units 5. Programme for strengthening export corporation 6. Entrepreneural development programme.	1. Construction of industrial estates. 2. Industrial fair 3. Assistance to handicraft societies 4. Assistance of working capital to industrial cooperatives.
Roads and Transportation	
1. Rennovation of district roads, bridges and culverts.	1. Construction of rural roads under Minimum Needs Programme.
Education	
1. Strengthening of district education administration. 2. Extension of secondary schools 3. Financial assistance to backward class students. 4. Innovative methods for curriculam.	1. Expansion of Primary education in districts.

(Contd.)

State Sector	District Sector
Health and Medical Care	
1. Establishment of Aurvedic/Unani dispensaries.	1. Establishment of additional primary health centres.
2. Programme for epidemic disease prevention.	2. Strengthening of Primary Health Centres.
Labour Welfare	
1. Strengthening of additional labour courts.	1. Rehabilitation of bonded labour.
Panchayat Raj	
1. Training for government and non-government panchayat officials.	1. Programme on technical and managerial assistance to panchayat industries.
	2. Development of rural markets.
Community Development	
1. Organising seminars, workshops for the members of youth-clubs of state and blocks.	1. Employment for rural youth
	2. Training camps for rural youth
2. Organisation of rural tournaments.	3. Promotion of cultural activities.
Cooperation	
1. Investment of share capital in cooperative credit institutions.	1. Interest free loan to the cooperative societies of scheduled caste tribes.
2. Training for Secretaries of Primary Agri. Credit societies	2. Margin money for foodgrains marketing through farmers service societies.
3. Plan for construction of Rural Godowns through World Bank aid	3. Margin money for primary consumer stores managed by women youth and students.
4. Establishment of rice and Dhal mills	
5. Rennovation of cold storage	
6. Subsidy for farm and non-farm consumer stores.	
Electricity	
1. New plants for electricity production.	1. Rural electrification.
2. Rural electrification.	

JAMMU AND KASHMIR

In this state the schemes having relevance to the whole district are included in the district level schemes. The projects which spread over more than one block like district highways, irrigation projects within command area spreading over more than one block, district and sub-district hospitals also figure in the district level schemes. In addition to this the projects eventhough located in one block but the benefits from which flow to other blocks are also included in the district sector schemes. Altogether, there are 38 items included in the list of district sector schemes. (Table 3.10).

There are certain schemes which are essentially required to be planned and executed at the state level and therefore, such schemes have been included in the state sector. The schemes like research, training and higher education are examples of this category. The schemes and programmes which are the responsibility of government corporations and companies and government departments are also included in the state level schemes whereas projects physically spread over more than one district like major irrigation projects, electric and transmission lines are also state level schemes. Similarly, the schemes located in one district but the benefit from which flows to other districts in the normal course such schemes are also included in the state sector. Tourism development projects and important bridges on state highways are some of the examples of schemes of this nature.

Table 3.10
District Sector Schemes—Jammu and Kashmir

Sl. No.	*Name of Sector*
1.	Agriculture
2.	Horticulture
3.	Applied Nutrition programme
4.	Massive Assistance to small and marginal farmers
5.	Soil & water conservation
6.	Animal husbandry
7.	Sheep Husbandry
8.	Fisheries

(Contd.)

Sl. No.	Name of Sector
9.	Forestry
10.	Storage and ware housing
11.	Cooperation
12.	I.R.D.P.
13.	N.R.E.P.
14.	Land reforms
15.	C.D. & Panchayats
16.	Gujjar & Bakarwal
17.	Minor irrigation
18.	Flood control
19.	Power/R.E.C.
20.	Handicrafts
21.	Handlooms
22.	DIC
23.	Sericulture
24.	Weights & Measures
25.	Roads & Bridges
26.	State Motor Garages
27.	General Education
28.	Health
29.	P.H.E.
30.	Housing
31.	Urban development
32.	S.C. & O.B.C.
33.	Labour welfare
34.	Self Employment
35.	Social welfare
36.	Nutrition
37.	Stationery and supplies
38.	P.W.D. (NFB)

WEST BENGAL

In West Bengal, besides state level, the district, block and gram panchayats have also been entrusted with certain schemes for planning

Table 3.11
District Sector Schemes - West Bengal

Sl. No.	Name of Sector
1.	Agriculture including Soil conservation and Agricultural Marketing
2.	Minor irrigation
3.	Irrigation and waterways
4.	Animal Husbandry
5.	Veterinary services
6.	Fisheries
7.	C & SSI including Sericulture, Handloom Biogas etc.
8.	Forests
9.	Roads
10.	Co-operation
11.	Education including Primary, Secondary Social Education & Library
12.	Youth Services and Sports
13.	Rural Electrification
14.	Special programme for Tribes
15.	Health & Family Welfare (excluding Central programme)
16.	Panchayat
17.	Community Development
18.	Public Health (PHE and Rural Sanitation)
19.	Local Govt. (Municipality)
20.	Tourism
21.	Social welfare
22.	P.W.D. & construction Board
23.	Rural Housing other than C.D.
24.	Housing (Rental & Loan)

and execution. In the district level schemes 25 sectors have been included consisting of agriculture, irrigation, animal husbandry, forestry, rural electrification, tribal development, rural housing besides the schemes for social services like health and education (Table 3.11). At the block level, the panchayat samithies have been empowered to execute certain schemes upto the estimated value of Rs. 50,000 whereas the Gram Panchayats deal with certain schemes with estimated cost of less than Rs. 5000.[6]

A review of decentralisation of functions for purposes of micro level planning has revealed that there are a few states which have taken steps to identify in addition to state sector schemes, district/block sector schemes also.

The point which emerges out of the cross country analysis of the schemes listed out as State, District, Sub-division, Block/Taluka and Mandal level is that the items included vary from state to state. If the classification of schemes and sectors is made strictly on the basis of technical feasibility of its planning and implementation at different levels, there is not much scope for this diversity among different states. It leads to the conclusion that the classification of schemes have scope for further revision on the basis of a rational analysis. In some states justification given for retaining certain schemes at the state level is that it requires constant technical supervision. At this formative stage it may be a right step but as the competence of the implementing agencies at the local level increases, out of their experience, even such activities can be safely passed on to the local agencies.

Notes and References

1. Gopalkrishnan, M., Status report on Decentralised planning and involvement of people in planning process in Andhra Pradesh, National seminar on Decentralised planning Feb. 13-14, 1988, State Planning Institute, Lucknow, p. 11.
2. Barua, Bhaskar, op. cit., p. 2.
3. Govt. of Bihar, Abstract statement of outlay sanctioned for identified district sector schemes in 1986-87, Part I, planning and development department, Patna, 1986.
4. Rajan, M.P., op. cit., p. 4-5.
5. State Planning Institute, U.P. Background paper for the seminar on Decentralised planning, 1988, p. 12.
6. Sarkar, Bikram, op. cit., p. 9.

2. Jha, Bhaskar, op cit., p 2.

4. Gupta, M.P., op cit, p 4-5.

6. Sarkar, Dinesh, op cit., p 9.

IV

Devolution of Financial Resources

The disaggregation of state plan outlays for districts and other lower units on rational basis is quite essential for making micro level planning a fruitful exercise. The state governments have realised its importance and hence accepted the basic idea of disaggregation of state plan outlay into state sector outlay and district sector outlay.

It may be observed that the division of the state plan outlays into state and district sector outlays depend upon the number of schemes listed out at these levels. In Gujarat 65 per cent and in Uttar Pradesh 70 per cent of the total outlay of the state plan is earmarked for state sector plan and the remaining 35 per cent and 30 per cent respectively are earmarked for district sectors. The district sector outlay so arrived at is redistributed among different districts on the basis of some variants of Gadgil formula. The outlay thus arrived at for each district is distributed among different sectors/sub-divisions/blocks/mandals as the case may be.

The district sector outlay available for micro level planning can be classified into three categories. These are (i) outlays for normal district level schemes tied up with the ongoing programmes and to be implemented as per the guidelines of the Central and State governments, (ii) 'discretionary outlays' or 'untied funds' which can be utilised by the local agency for implementing schemes/programmes of local importance selected by them, and (iii) incentive outlay to be allocated against some matching funds raised by the local agency for implementing schemes of their choice. In some of the states the district planning agency has also been empowered to reallocate the fund earmarked for normal district level schemes from one sector to another depending on the requirement. This power for reappropriation is however, very limited.

The state-wise picture of the financial decentralisation for micro level planning has been presented in the succeeding pages.

ANDHRA PRADESH

Allocation of Fund

The district segments of financial allocation in this state is worked out by dividing the total state plan outlay into divisible and non-divisible outlays. The divisible outlays include allocation under all such schemes, the benefits of which accrue to the concerned district only. The non-divisible outlay which would benefit more than one district are kept aside to be operated by the state level departments. These include outlays on major and medium irrigation, major industries, state level corporations, state highways and power generation. For programmes like IRDP, DPAP, NREP, RLEGP and Minimum Needs Programme, the Government of India guidelines are followed in working out the district segments.

On the basis of this exercise, in 1987-88 Rs. 523.8 crores constituting 34.0 per cent of outlay was earmarked from state's funds for distribution among the districts. Further, Rs. 190.20 crores provided as central share was added to the divisible outlay making a total of Rs. 714 crores (46.4% of total outlay Rs. 1540 crores) (Table 4.1). The Central assistance was provided for IRDP, DPAP, NREP, RLEGP, crop husbandry, village industries, rural water supply, welfare of SC, ST population etc.

As can be seen from Table 4.2 out of Rs. 523.80 crores of state's share in the divisible pool, about 58 per cent is allotted to social services, about 12 per cent to rural development programmes, 9 per cent to agricultural schemes and the rest to irrigation and flood control, energy, industry and minerals and transport. It can be seen from Table 4.1 that out of Rs. 190.20 crores shown as Centre's share, about 31 per cent is allotted to social services and about 62 per cent to rural development and the rest to village industries, water supply etc.

Table 4.1
Annual Plan Outlays of State and Centre, 1987-88

(Rs. in Lakhs)

S. No.	Head of Development	State Share: Annual Plan provision	State Share: Divisible outlay	Percentage	Central share of outlay	Total divisible Plan (4+6)	Percentage of state share
1	2	3	4	5	6	7	8
I.	**Agriculture and Allied Services**	6669.000	2795.630	41.92	991.950	3787.580	73.8
a.	Crop Husbandry	1764.000	1504.980	85.32	769.090	2274.070	66.2
b.	Soil and Water Conservation	105.000	66.300	62.86	-	66.300	100.0
c.	Animal Husbandry	730.000	616.590	84.46	5.060	621.650	99.2
d.	Dairy development	200.000	103.000	51.50	-	103.000	100.0
e.	Fisheries	750.000	428.250	57.10	115.300	543.550	78.8
f.	Marketing	129.000	76.510	59.31	102.500	179.010	42.7
g.	Others	2991.000	-	-		-	-
II.	**Rural Development**	6163.060	6132.785	99.51	11771.705	17904.490	34.2
a.	I.R.D.P.	2846.560	2570.485	90.30	2570.485	5140.970	50.0
b.	D.P.A.P.	517.500	455.675	80.05	455.675	911.350	50.0
c.	N.R.E.P.	2439.000	3106.625	127.37	3106.625	6213.250	50.0
d.	R.L.E.G.P.	-	-	-	5638.920	5638.920	-
e.	Others	360.000	-	-	-	-	-
III.	**Special Area Development Programme**	14.500	-	-	-	-	-
IV.	**Irrigation and Flood Control**	51250.000	2567.810	25.87	-	2567.810	100.0
a.	Major and medium	47850.00	-	-	-	-	-
b.	Minor irrigation	2300.000	2567.810	111.64	-	2567.810	100.0
c.	Command Area development	600.000	-	-	-	-	-
d.	Others	500.00	-	-	-	-	-

(Contd.)

1	2	3	4	5 .	6	7	8
V.	**Energy**	26535.000	5500.000	20.72	-	5500.000	100.0
a.	Andhra Pradesh S.E.B.	25000.000	5500.000	22.000	-	5500.000	100.0
b.	Others	1535.000	-	-	-	-	-
VI.	**Industry and Minerals**	6223.890	336.955	5.41	179.805	516.760	65.2
a.	Village and small industries	2127.890	288.275	13.55	179.805	468.080	61.6
b.	Large and Medium	3036.000	48.690	1.60	-	48.680	100.0
c.	Others	1060.000	-	-	-		
VII.	**Transport**	7384.000	2205.330	29.87	-	2205.330	100.0
a.	Mini Ports and Light Houses	175.000	175.000	100.00	-	175.000	100.0
b.	Roads & Bridges	3025.000	1983.830	65.58	-	1983.830	100.0
c.	Traffic control	98.000	46.500	47.45	-	46.500	100.0
d.	Others	4086.000	-	-	-	-	-
VIII.	**Communications**	-	-	-	-	-	-
IX.	**Science Technology and Environment**	201.000	-	-	-	-	-
X.	**General Economic Services**	583.690	125.210	21.45	136.750	261.960	47.8
a.	Economic Advice and statistics	100.000	114.210	114.21	136.750	250.960	45.5
b.	Tourism	325.000	11.000	3.38	-	11.000	100.0
c.	Others	158.690	-	-	-	-	-
XI.	**Social Services**	46635.580	30805.475	66.05	5940.525	36746.000	83.8
a.	General Education	8165.750	5318.540	65.13	392.050	5710.590	93.1
b.	Sports and Youth services	148.000	11.590	7.83	-	11.590	100.0
c.	Technical Education	516.000	494.600	95.85	-	494.600	100.0
d.	Art & culture	134.000	76.710	57.25	-	76.710	100.0
e.	Medical & Public Health	3345.000	1167.630	34.91	-	1167.630	100.0
f.	Water supply and sanitation	7900.000	6933.980	87.77	1991.750	8925.730	77.7

1	2	3	4	5	6	7	8
g.	Housing	7600.580	5660.000	74.30	-	5660.000	100.0
h.	Urban development	3845.000	1305.000	42.06	50.000	1355.000	96.3
i.	Welfare of scheduled tribe and backward classes	12865.000	8930.705	68.88	1687.965	18618.670	84.1
j.	Labour and employment	480.500	269.000	39.53	-	269.000	100.0
k.	Social security & welfare	1618.750	637.720	39.39	1818.760	2456.400	26.0
l.	Others	689.000	-	-	-		-
XII.	**General Services**	**2368.030**	**1910.000**	**80.66**	**-**	**1919.000**	**100.0**
a.	Stationery and printing	15.000	15.000	100.00	-	15.000	100.00
b.	Chief Engineer buildings	1223.030	895.000	73.18	-	895.000	100.00
c.	Mandal buildings	1000.000	1000.000	100.00	-	1000.000	100.00
d.	Others	130.000	-	-	-	-	-
	Grand Total	154027.750	52379.195	34.01	19020.735	71399.930	73.4

For allocation of divisible fund among the districts the following factors have been identified:

1. Total population
2. SC population
3. ST population
4. Geographical area
5. Gaps in social infrastructure
6. Drought affected areas
7. Length to sea coast
8. Needs of supplementary employment programme.

Table 4.2

State's share of divisible pool Annual Plan Outlay 1987-88 by Districts

Rs. lakhs

S. No.	District	I. Agri. & allied service	II. Rural Development	III. Special area development programme	IV. Irrigation & flood control	V. Energy	VI. Industry Minerals	VII. Transport
1.	Srikakulam	117.605	264.095	-	80.000	310.800	15.020	43.470
2.	Vizianagaram	90.390	304.280	-	340.700	219.300	10.150	73.180
3.	Visakhapatnam	98.450	257.130	-	290.390	426.850	11.355	76.680
4.	East Godavari	19.645	338.525	-	40.550	231.500	17.700	164.200
5.	West Godavari	97.470	286.245	-	34.400	200.400	24.250	157.110
6.	Krishna	86.820	292.485	-	51.190	187.400	17.710	280.670
7.	Guntur	122.995	351.920	-	51.660	172.600	25.215	109.810
8.	Prakasam	169.790	338.415	-	143.270	208.800	12.400	64.440
9.	Nellore	167.630	240.150	-	97.220	167.100	13.230	56.620
Coastal Andhra Region		**1070.795**	**2673.245**	**-**	**1129.380**	**2124.750**	**147.30**	**1026.180**
10.	Kurnool	154.725	316.960	-	183.520	185.500	13.965	86.050
11.	Anantapur	149.680	381.845	-	155.230	220.400	14.430	32.490
12.	Cuddapah	142.345	229.715	-	99.470	135.950	10.000	58.520
13.	Chittoor	110.855	363.925	-	147.300	232.550	32.400	65.860
Rayalaseema Region		**557.605**	**1292.445**	**-**	**585.520**	**774.400**	**70.795**	**242.920**
14.	Rangareddy	178.685	170.500	-	114.650	125.000	10.205	18.490
15.	Hyderabad	43.430	-	-	-	1107.250	6.620	139.930
16.	Nizamabad	58.965	157.290	-	56.020	123.150	19.945	102.220
17.	Medak	95.715	192.920	-	117.570	141.200	10.670	47.290
18.	Mahabubnagar	124.635	350.820	-	126.450	170.150	13.470	94.710
19.	Nalgonda	145.800	290.325	-	72.380	171.350	13.300	161.290
20.	Warangal	140.845	272.205	-	78.710	174.950	11.740	116.030
21.	Khammam	116.410	245.310	-	87.890	171.150	9.860	63.410
22.	Karimnagar	130.275	279.930	-	89.160	188.800	12.110	59.840
23.	Adilabad	132.470	207.795	-	110.080	227.850	11.210	133.020
Telangana Region		**1167.230**	**2167.095**	**-**	**852.910**	**2600.850**	**119.130**	**936.230**
Total Andhra Pradesh		***2795.630***	***6132.785***	***-***	***2567.810***	***5500.000***	***336.955***	***2205.330***

VIII. Communication	IX. Science Technology and Environment	X. General Economic Services	XI. Social Services	XII. General Services	Grand Total
—	—	4.410	927.045	35.000	1798.045
—	—	4.160	974.485	64.000	2080.645
—	—	4.510	2168.805	33.000	3367.170
—	—	6.050	1640.505	52.000	2610.675
—	—	4.860	1077.710	35.000	1917.445
—	—	4.760	1225.185	56.000	2202.220
—	—	4.830	1327.140	47.000	2213.170
—	—	5.180	1205.360	95.000	2242.655
—	—	4.770	1127.605	35.000	1909.325
—	**—**	**43.530**	**11674.440**	**452.000**	**20341.350**
—	—	5.330	1204.060	69.500	2219.610
—	—	7.540	1248.540	42.000	2252.155
—	—	7.230	931.090	160.000	1774.320
—	—	10.510	1196.885	51.000	2211.285
—	**—**	**30.610**	**4580.575**	**322.500**	**8457.370**
—	—	4.750	935.325	44.000	1601.605
—	—	3.410	4677.395	686.500	6664.535
—	—	4.720	798.275	29.000	1349.585
—	—	5.150	857.725	35.000	1483.240
—	—	6.830	1045.465	55.000	1987.530
—	—	5.360	1285.705	45.000	2190.510
—	—	5.010	1335.315	100.000	2234.805
—	—	5.010	1361.055	39.000	2099.095
—	—	5.360	937.030	61.000	1763.505
—	—	5.470	1337.170	41.000	2206.065
—	**—**	**51.070**	**14550.46**	**1135.500**	**23850.475**
—	**—**	**125.210**	**30805.475**	**1910.000**	**52379.195**

Untied Funds

During 1984-85, an amount of Rs. 23 crores at the rate of Rs. 1 crore to each district was allocated in the nature of untied funds to help finance 'crucial balancing investment'. This scheme contemplates full utilisation of capital assets created already either under plan or non-plan or any other contingent plan, the works undertaken under this scheme were non-recurring nature.[1] The district planning boards were given full freedom in the selection and approval of schemes under this provision. The other innovation is the new schemes called "Telugu Grameena Kranthi Patham". Under this scheme 50 per cent of the value of the work done irrespective of the cost of materials and labour are paid by the Government. During 1985-86 Rs. 1100 lakhs was released as assistance to districts. In 1986-87 and 1987-88 the provisions were Rs. 755.3 lakhs and 878 lakhs respectively. During 1988-89 an amount of Rs. 595 lakhs was released upto December 1988. These funds were released to various Mandals/Assembly segments as per the requirements. This is a scheme for execution of a large number of small works as listed out in the countryside not requiring substantial skills, but locally relevant and significant which reflects felt needs of the people and executed directly by the people through "Telugu Shrama Dalams". Under this programme the following types of the schemes are taken up: (1) Construction and maintenance of drainage and minor irrigation works including community irrigation wells and individual irrigation wells, bores for SCs, STs, BCs and economically backward classes, (2) Formation and upgradation of village roads, (3) improvements to the public assets like school buildings, PHC buildings, public parks, school play grounds, (4) provision of community latrines, (5) afforestation programme and planting fruit bearing sapplings in backyards, (6) protected water supply schemes, (7) buildings for milk collection centres. The criteria for selection and execution of works under this programme are as follows:

(1) the estimated cost of each scheme should not exceed Rs. 5 lakhs

(2) 50 per cent of the cost of work done shall be paid by the government

(3) the labour component should be free and voluntary from the local people.

ASSAM

Allocation of Fund

In this state 20% of the total allocation of the state has been earmarked for decentralised planning. Out of this amount 10% has been set apart as untied amount. Out of the remaining 90%, 50% has been distributed to different sub-divisions on the basis of the weightage assigned to the following factors.[2]

1. Total population 50%
2. Geographical area 20%
3. Scheduled tribe population 13%
4. Scheduled caste population 7%

The state government has also adopted a new approach. Generally the performance in the past regarding the implementation of different schemes pertaining to different sectors or in other words, the financial achievements of different sectors in the past are the basis for arriving at the sectoral allocation. In this state the sectoral size is determined on the basis of various criteria evolved. Some of the criteria adopted for determining the sectoral size for each sub-division are outlined below.[3]

(1) agriculture - net sown area;
(2) animal husbandry - cattle population;
(3) fisheries - water areas;
(4) panchayat - number of gram panchayats;
(5) cooperation - number of primary agriculture cooperatives;
(6) handloom - number of weaving cooperative societies;
(7) sericulture - number of families engaged in sericulture;
(8) education - backlog in education;
(9) health - population;
(10) water supply - village having no water supply facilities;
(11) roads - deficiency in respect of roads per 100 sq. km.
(12) land reforms - ceiling surplus land to be distributed.

This criteria seem to be very rational as on one side it takes care of the scope or potentiality for development of that sector and secondly, it will lead to the balanced development of different sectors and different pockets in the district.

Untied Fund

Out of the total fund available for decentralised planning as mentioned earlier, 10% is reserved as untied fund. This amount has been kept aside for distribution by government to those sub-divisions which require such allocation for meeting special problems. A sum of Rs. 11 crores was allocated as untied fund for the year 1987-88. For 1988-89, the amount under this head has been increased to Rs. 12 crores.

Power of Re-appropriation

At present neither separate budget is prepared nor a separate budget head exists for schemes under sub-divisional plan. The Deputy Commissioners are not empowered to reappropriate the fund from one sector to other.

In 1986-87, the district sector outlay was increased to 34.11% out of which the untied fund constitutes 12.5% (Table 4.3).

Table 4.3

Outlay under Major Head of Development of District Sector Schemes 1986-87

(Rs. in lakhs)

	Major Head of Development	District sector schemes 1986-87	
		Total outlay	District sector outlay
I.	Agriculture and allied services	18877.75	18716.34
II.	Cooperation	103.00	103.00
III.	Water and power development	167.10	157.10
IV.	Industries and Minerals	410.00	349.11
V.	Transport and communication	4674.58	4544.58
VI.	Social and community services	10527.13	10356.41
	Total	34759.06	34226.54
(A)	Percentage of District Sector outlay to total outlay (i.e. 1150 crores)		29.76%
VII.	Miscellaneous District planning (Untied fund)	5000.00	5000.00
	Grand Total	39759.06	39226.54
(B)	Percentage of Dist. sector outlay to total outlay (1150 crores)		34.11%

BIHAR

Allocation of Fund

The total plan outlay of the state is distributed between state sector and district sector schemes. It was decided that 30 per cent of the state plan outlay in each annual plan would be allotted for district sector schemes during the period of the Seventh Five-year Plan. Out of this 30 per cent, 24 per cent would be earmarked for district sector schemes submitted by the departments of government and six per cent would be untied funds. Government have now decided to increase the outlay for district sector schemes from 30 per cent to 40 per cent. This includes the untied fund of 10 per cent.

Untied Fund

To enable the district planning and development councils to take up schemes at their own initiatives, within the guidelines laid down by the government, the untied funds are distributed among the districts on the basis of approved formula i.e. 60 per cent on the basis of population, 30% on backwardness and 10% on special problems. Further breakup of these criteria are—

(a) Population

  i. total population - 40%
  ii. urban population - 5%
  iii. population of SC/ST - 10%
  iv. population of small farmers/marginal farmers/landless labourers - 5%

(b) Backwardness in

  i. agriculture - 5%
  ii. irrigation - 5%
  iii. industries - 5%
  iv. rural electrification - 5%
  v. drinking water facilities - 5%
  vi. communication - 5%

The untied fund available during 1986-87 was Rs. 50 crores. (Table 4.4) for the year 1987-88 the amount has been further raised to Rs. 74.76 crores. For 1988-89 an amount of Rs. 120.78 crores has been earmarked for this purpose to be distributed among 39 districts. Thus at an average Rs. 3 crores per district is available as untied fund.

GUJARAT

Allocation of Fund

In the Sixth Plan, against a total allocation of Rs. 3760 crores, allocation for district level schemes was Rs. 1517 crores (40%). In the Seventh Plan the corresponding figures are Rs. 6000 crores and Rs. 2450 crores respectively (40.8%).

In this state it has been decided to allocate 35% of the State Plan outlays on an average for district level schemes during the period of five year plan.[4] In practice even more than 40% of the state plan outlays have been utilised for district level schemes. Out of this amount available for district level schemes, 20 per cent is provided to District planning boards. Out of this 20 per cent 15% is discretionary outlay and 5% as incentive grant. The remaining 80 per cent of the district sector

Table 4.4

Sector-wise Allocation of Funds in Gujarat

S. No.	Head of Deptt.	Sixth Five Year Plan (1980-85) All Plan schemes			Performance (Rs. in lakhs) District level scheme		
		Outlay	Expnd.	Percentage	Outlay	Expend.	Percentage
I.	Agriculture & Allied Services	36773.00	41818.68	113.72	29675.90	32464.60	109.40
II.	Cooperation	3200.00	4580.85	143.14	1953.60	794.25	40.66
III.	Irrigation & Power	207161.00	195875.30	94.55	48925.55	57945.06	118.49
IV.	Industries & Minerals	1740.00	22276.81	130.20	5852.00	8991.22	145.10
V.	Transport & Communication	33860.00	39455.85	116.53	22000.00	25379.09	115.36
VI.	Social & Community services	57316.00	67720.70	118.15	23161.44	32058.61	138.41
VII.	Economic Services	580.00	537.43	92.66	135.75	95.25	143.83
VIII.	Decentralised District Planning	20000.00	16916.00	84.58	20000.00	16916.00	84.58
	Total	276000.00	388681.61	103.37	151704.24	174244.08	114.86

scheme outlay is for normal district level schemes which are implemented through the District Level Heads of Departments. Almost the entire state outlay on programmes of rural development like IRDP, NREP, DPAP etc. are treated as outlays for normal district level schemes and are taken into account within the 80% of the district sector scheme. During the Sixth Plan period for district level schemes there was a provision of Rs. 1517 crores out of the total outlay of Rs. 3,760 crores for the state. The sectorwise breakup of allocation and achievement can be seen from Table 4.4.

The district plan funds are distributed among districts on the basis of a formula which takes into account various criteria to which weightage would be given as in Table 4.5.[5]

Table 4.5
Criteria for Allocation of Funds Among Districts in Gujarat

S.No.	*Item*	*Percentage*
1.	Population (excluding towns having population of 50,000 and above)	40
2.	Population of scheduled castes and scheduled tribes and small and marginal farmers and population of agricultural labourers other than scheduled castes and scheduled tribes.	15
3.	Agricultural backwardness	10
4.	Irrigational backwardness	10
5.	Industrial backwardness	5
6.	Backwardness in respect of roads and drinking water	10
7.	Backwardness in respect of the targets of other selected minimum needs	5
8.	Incentive provision	5
	Total	100

In computing the population for the purpose of this formula, only rural population and population of towns with less than 50,000 people are taken into account. This is because the focus of decentralised planning is mainly on the rural areas and the small towns, although allocations to cities and larger towns are not ruled out.

Untied Fund

As already mentioned, 20% of the District Plan outlay consists of discretionary and incentive outlay. These are placed at the discretion of D.P.B. to take up schemes of local importance. "The DPB can finance projects on 100% basis from the discretionary component of the District Plan outlay".[6] While the incentive outlay requires a matching contribution of 50% or 25% depending upon the pattern prescribed for the taluka. The latter 25 per cent contribution from the local level and 75 per cent from the state is applicable to relatively backward talukas. These areas are by and large included in (1) Drought Prone Area Programme, (2) Desert Development Programme, (3) Tribal Area Sub-plan, and (4) 25 backward talukas based on the Hathi Samithi Report. The remaining talukas are entitled to 50 per cent matching contribution for incentive outlay from the state. Taking the state as a whole, the ratio between the amount sanctioned by the Government for incentive outlay and the amount mobilised by people has been 3:2.

With effect from 1982-83 the District Planning Boards have started allocating at least 67% to 75% of their discretionary outlay among different talukas in the proportion as determined by the criteria mentioned below. The remaining 25 to 33 per cent of the discretionary outlay is retained at the district level for schemes benefiting more than one taluka.

1. Population of taluka excluding the population of town having population of 50,000 or more.
2. Population of SC/ST and agricultural labourers excluding those belong to SC/ST.
3. Backwardness in agriculture with reference to the following parameters:
   - (a) Proportion of cultivable area to the toal geographical area;
   - (b) Proportion of cultivated area to the cultivable area;
   - (c) Proportion of area under irrigation to total cropped area;
   - (d) Proportion of area sown more than once to the total cropped area;
   - (e) Proportion of area under major cash crops to the total cropped area;
   - (f) Proportion of cropped area per agricultural workers.
   - (g) Proportion of cultivable area per agricultural workers.

4. Irrigational backwardness as measured with reference to the proportion of the area which does not receive the benefit of irrigation from out of total cropped area of the taluka.

5. Industrial backwardness as measured with reference to the percentage of average numbers of workers daily employed by the industrial units to the total number of workers in the taluka.

6. Backwardness in road, as measured with reference to the number of villages which are not connected by Pucca roads as also the population of such villages.

7. Backwardness in the field of drinking water supply as measured with reference to the number of villages without having any facilities for drinking water supply.

8. Backwardness in the field of education as measured with reference to the following parameters:

   (a) number of villages having no primary schools,

   (b) population of such villages, and

   (c) number of additional school rooms required with reference to the existing criteria of the education department.

9. Backwardness in the field of rural public health as measured with regard to:

   (a) the number of primary health centre and sub-centres to be opened according to the norms envisaged for the MP in the Sixth Plan document;

   (b) population of such villages, and

   (c) the number of villages electrified for agricultural purpose only.

A Taluka Level Committee has been set-up to formulate proposals against the outlay allocated to them.

As regards to the 20 per cent outlay placed at the disposal of the DPB, it has been authorised to take up schemes costing not more than Rs. 10 lakhs. Guidelines have also been issued from the state government that no allocation can be made for schemes of non-developmental nature like replacement of old vehicles by new one, purchase of stationery, office equipment, construction of office buildings etc. Instructions are also there to ensure adequate fund for minimum needs programme and particularly schemes which benefit SC and ST population.

During the sixth plan period a total amount of Rs. 171.44 crores was allocated to district planning boards. Rs. 131.36 crores as discretionary outlay and Rs. 40.08 as incentive outlay. Out of this Rs. 169.16 crores were disbursed by them for various projects. This amount was utilised for implementation of 59,644 schemes of local importance. Priority was assigned to Minimum Needs Programme and about 74% of the total allocation was spent on this programme (Table 4.6)

Table 4.6
Allocations made by DPB on MNP in Gujarat during Sixth Plan period.

Rs. in lakhs

Programme	*Allocation*	*Percentage*
I. Minimum Needs Programme		
(a) Rural Electrification	664.57	4.2
(b) Rural Roads	4489.94	28.3
(c) Elementary Education	2768.12	17.5
(d) Adult Education	0.26	-
(e) Rural Health	664.51	4.1
(f) Rural Water supply	2627.55	16.6
(g) Rural Housing	132.01	0.8
(h) Environmental Improvement of slums	97.34	0.6
(i) Nutrition	38.71	0.2
(j) Mid-day meal programme	262.41	1.7
Total : I MNP	11725.42	74.0
II. Programme other than MNP	4115.27	26.0
Total	*15840.69	100.0

* Exclusive of allocation of Rs. 539.80 lakhs for Integrated Programme for urban poor, Rs. 216.05 lakhs for development of special backward areas and Rs. 320.32 lakhs for construction of Primary School rooms.

As the discretionary and incentive allocations have been provided for the implementation of schemes of local importance, these have generated popular enthusiasm. Suggestions for new works keep pouring into the District planning offices. Due to popular interest public contribution against incentive outlay is also forthcoming. During the sixth plan period, people's contribution was 94.5 per cent of the amount required to be raised against the incentive outlay.

Certain areas of the state, due to special geographical features, have special problems of backwardness and cannot be covered by the normal District Plan allocation, ten such areas have been identified and special outlays provided to the District Planning Boards for undertaking schemes to benefit those areas. The Government had also set up a committee headed by an eminent economist of international reputation to help in identifying the backward areas of the state and evolving a strategy of their balanced development.

HIMACHAL PRADESH
Financial Allocation

Financial decentralisation has been introduced since 1984-85 in respect of Tribal sub-plan in the state. At an average 9 per cent of the total state plan outlay has been earmarked for the tribal sub-plan. This has been distributed to the five ITDPs constituting the tribal sub-plan area in the state based on some criteria. This process facilitates determination of sectoral priorities under tribal sub-plan in a more realistic way.

The State Government has decided to set aside fund for the implementation of district sector schemes after the list of such schemes are ready. The level of outlays to be exclusively earmarked for district planning would be determined based on the actuals on such schemes for the past 2-3 years. The level of outlay would remain fixed for a period of five years. This will be revised for the next five year plan based on the actual requirement of the schemes to be implemented at district level.

With regard to inter-district allocation of earmarked resources the State Government is thinking to adopt a rational formula which would, by and large, be on the pattern adopted by the UP Government.

Untied Fund

In the process of decentralisation of plan in Himachal Pradesh, the concept of untied funds for district planning has been introduced for 10 districts except tribal area. This amount is to be utilised by the Deputy Commissioners on the recommendations of district planning and development committee. This allocation is meant for local development works of important nature for which adequate normal and specific provisions are not available in the budget. The allocation of this fund among the districts is made according to a formula which gives 60 per cent weightage to population and 40 per cent to area. In 1985-86 an outlay of Rs. 100 lakhs was provided as untied funds and the provisions for 1987-88 was Rs. 375 lakhs. For 1988-89 Rs. 375 lakhs has been recommended. The districtwise break-up of allocation of funds under local district planning for the year 1988-89 is shown in Table 4.7. Each scheme to be sanctioned under the local development works are supposed to benefit atleast five households. The maximum limit of expenditure from the resources provided for local development works for any individual scheme is to be limited to Rs. 25,000. These schemes are such which do not create any recurring liability.

Budget for Construction of Primary School Buildings

There is a separate provision for this purpose. The funds are allotted to the district on the basis of needs of the district with a view to provide this facility in each district for a balanced growth of these institutions.

JAMMU AND KASHMIR

Financial Allocation

The present procedure of determining the district outlays in the state is that once the plan outlays for the state are settled and sectoral provisions and priorities determined, the Heads of the Departments are required to communicate the break-up of state sector component and the district sector component of their sectoral plans according to the existing guidelines issued by the State Government. The proportion of the district sector component thus arrived at is distributed amongst the districts on the basis of three broad guiding factors viz., population, area and level of development or backwardness. The proportion of district sector component in the total state plan does not remain constant but varies from year to year. On an average, 40% to 45% of the total state plan is earmarked for district sector schemes every year.[7]

Table 4.7
Allocation of Funds District-wise for Local District Planning (Himachal Pradesh)

S.No.	Name of the district	Allocation during 1984-85 LDP	1985-86 LDP	1986-87 LDP	1987-88 LDP
1.	Bilaspur	1,00,640	2,02,280	2,51,600	21,09 000
2.	Chamba	1,55,440	3,10,880	3,88,600	30,76,000
3.	Hampur	1,19,920	2,39,840	2,99,800	11,45,000
4.	Kangra	4,30,040	8,60,080	10,75,100	38,23,000
5.	Kulu	2,06,640	4,13,280	5,16,600	24,33,000
'6.	Mandi	2,85,440	5,70,880	7,13,600	31,01,000
7.	Sixmur	1,59,360	3,18,720	3,98,400	15,44,000
8.	Solan	1,36,240	2,72,480	3,40,600	21,63,000
9.	Shimli	2,76,000	5,52,000	6,90,000	40,44,000
10.	Una	1,30,280	2,60,560	3,25,700	11,97,000
11.	Kinnaur	-	-	-	5,00,000
12.	Lahaul and Spiti	-	-	-	5,00,000
13.	Total	20,00,000	40,00,000	50,00,000	2,56,35,000

Once the Planning Department communicates to each district development commissioner the total outlay for the District Plan together with sectoral break-up as well as broad priorities and guidelines, a detailed District Plan is drawn up by the District Administration in consultation with the District Development board. Since 1986-87 lumpsum outlays for five broad sectors of economy are being communicated to the District authorities on the basis of which District Development Boards apportion the outlays for each of the sectors and sub-sectors after taking into consideration the need, priorities and guidelines issued by Planning Department. These five broad sectors are as under:

i. Agriculture and Rural Development

ii. Industry and commerce

iii. Power

iv. Transport and communications

v. Social and community services.

Size of population and relative backwardness of the districts are the guiding factors for determining the district outlays, similarly the sum total of the outlays earmarked for the block level schemes under each sector/subsector in the light of the above guidelines constitute the block component of the district plan (Table 4.8) and the same is distributed amongst various blocks of the district on the basis of the following factors:

Table 4.8
Criteria for Allocation of Funds to Blocks

Criterion	Weight
a. size of population	40%
b. size of scheduled castes/ ST population	5%
c. population of recognised backward classes	5%
d. Geographical area	15%
e. Cropped area	15%
f. Livestock population	15%
g. Backwardness:	5%
i. Education-literacy %	
ii. Health-No. of sub-centres, dispensaries and other such centres (allopathic, ayurvedic unani per 1000 pop.)	
iii. Road length per 100 sq. km. of area	
iv. Area irrigated as percentage of net area sown	
v. Drinking water facilities-percentage of villages covered.	
Total	100%

With the introduction of this system, it is expected that the planning process in the state would be further rationalised and comparatively more backward areas will get preference and existing disparities amongst various area within a district, if any, would be removed.

Untied Fund

The suggestion of the Planning Commission, Government of India for providing 'untied grants' to the districts has been accepted by the state government and the same is proposed to be implemented from 1989-90. The State Government has accordingly proposed an outlay of Rs. 14.00 crores under the General Economic Services Planning Machinery 'Untied grants' during 1989-90 for distribution amongst the 14 districts, under the following two categories.

(i) Crucial Balancing Investment

50% of the outlay may be spent by the District Development Boards on such schemes so as to meet the felt local needs and aspirations which may not be otherwise provided or not fully accommodated in the State Plan. These outlays could also be partly utilised for balancing the outlays in any particular sector keeping in view the local requirements, potential and for providing missing links in the infrastructure etc. to make schemes functional ; and

(ii) Incentive Outlays

50% of the proposed outlays may be provided to the districts for generating people's contribution through incentive outlays. This scheme of local initiative besides involving community in the process of development, is likely to ensure generation of more resources for execution of development works in the district. The state is already implementing a scheme of construction of school building with public participation.

KARNATAKA

Financial Allocation

Earlier the state government used to allocate at an average about Rs. 2 crores for each district for spending on district sector schemes approved by the District Development Council. Due to the decentralised system now each district is receiving Rs. 30-40 crores. During 1987-88 in the state budget there was a provision for transfer of Rs. 950 crores to the Zilla Parishad and Mandal Panchayat. Out of the total allocation for district sector schemes 75 per cent of the allocation is distributed among 19 districts based on a 12-point formula. (Table 4.9). The remaining 25 per cent is kept with the state to be utilised in different districts for meeting their special problems.

Table 4.9
Criteria for Allocation of Fund Among Districts

Sl. No.	Indicator		Weight
1.	Population		50%
2.	Agricultural backwardness as measured by the value of agricultural output		5%
3.	Backwardness in irrigation as measured by proportion of irrigated area to net area sown		5%
4.	Backwardness as measured by the value of industrial output		5%
5.	Backwardness in communication as measured by road and railway length in kms. per 100 sq. km. area and per lakh population		2.1/2%
6.	Backwardness in financial infrastructure as measured by size of population served by each commercial and co-operative bank		2.1.2%
7.	Backwardness in medical and health facilities as measured by the number of hospitals per 1000 population/bed population ratio		5%
8.	Backwardness in power supply:		
	(a) As measured by the proportion of villages electrified	2.-1/2%	
	(b) Per capita power consumption	2.-1/2%	5%
9.	Problems of weaker sections:		
	(a) As measured by the proportion of SC/STs population	2.-1/2%	
	(b) As measured by the proportion of landless agricultural labour	2.-1/2%	5%
10.	Local tax effort		5%
11.	Special problems of Malnad areas and drought prone areas:		
	(a) As measured by the area under forests	2.-1/2%	
	(b) As measured by the rural population of drought-prone areas	2.-1/2%	5%
12.	Incidence of unemployment as measured by the proportion of registrants at the employment exchange.		5%

As population is a major factor which decides the burden that would be imposed on a region in terms of food requirements, infrastructural needs and employment requirements population has been given due consideration. These considerations explain the priority and weightage of 50 per cent assigned to population.

Infrastructural backwardness gets the priority next to population. Infrastructural development is a precondition for agricultural and industrial development and for optimum utilisation of resources. The responsibility of supplying infrastructural facilities falls on the shoulders of the public sector. This is the logic behind the high weightage of 20 per cent assigned to infrastructural facilities.

In an attempt to strengthen the special developmental efforts in districts facing the socio-economic problem of unemployment, special problems of weaker sections of society and the problems of hilly and drought prone areas, weightage of 5 per cent each has been given to these aspects.

The industrial and agricultural backwardness has also been taken as a factor for giving weightage, keeping in view the fact that a major effort in solving the problems in those sectors will have to come from the private sector.

It is necessary to ensure that resource mobilisation by the local bodies is directed towards achieving better development of the region. Unless this responsibility is accepted by the local bodies, the overall developmental effort will not be fruitful. With a view to making the local bodies conscious of what is expected from them and also introduce incentive schemes to spur them to maximum resource mobilisation effort, the criterion of local tax effort has been given an important place. If the local bodies fail to achieve the targets set for the district, the flow of funds from the state would get reduced.

On the basis of this formula for distribution of resources, the backward districts are allocated higher outlay compared to developed districts. Further formulation of location specific schemes and people's participation in the development process are also ensured.

Out of the total fund available for developmental activities in the district some amount is retained at the Zilla Parishad level itself and fund for taking up schemes benefiting more than one mandal panchayat are apportioned from the district level fund.

Each mandal panchayat is also given some fund directly from the state for implementation of such schemes which are beneficial to the mandal. This fund is distributed among the mandal panchayats, on the basis of the following formula.

1. Size of population 60%
2. Geographical area 15%
3. Extent of dry land 15%
4. Size of agricultural land 10%

At an average each mandal gets a minimum of Rs. 8 lakhs to a maximum of Rs. 20 lakhs. In Mysore district which consists of 165 mandal panchayats, during 1977-78, Rs. 2700 lakhs were approved. Out of this, Rs. 731 lakhs (25%) were for Zilla Parishad schemes including establishment charges for different departments. For mandal panchayat category I schemes Rs. 233 lakhs (10%) were earmarked and the balance of Rs. 1736 lakhs (65%) was meant for mandal panchayat category II schemes (i.e. schemes benefiting more than one mandal).

KERALA

Financial Allocation

With the decentralisation of formulation and implementation of schemes under special component plan to the district level from 1983-84 onwards there has been financial decentralisation also. There has been a provision for separate budget sub-heads of accounts for the funds earmarked for special component plan schemes of the different departments. Total investment of the order of Rs. 100 crores had been made during the sixth plan period for special component plan which was 5.72 per cent of the total plan expenditure of the state.

During 1987-88 the allocation to Special Component Plan was Rs. 69.61 crores which constituted 11.41 per cent (Table 4.10).

Table 4.10
Special component Plan for Scheduled Castes 1987-88
Flow of Funds—Summary Abstract

(Rs. in crores)

S. No.	Source	Outlay 1987-88	Flow to special component plan	Percentage to total outlay
1.	General sector (state share)	440.00	40.54	9.21
2.	Centrally sponsored schemes (central share)	155.99	24.57	15.65
3.	Special Central assistance	13.84	4.50	32.51
		609.88	69.61	11.41

In the Annual Plan nearly 40% of the total outlay is set apart for sectors like power development, large and medium industries, major and medium irrigation etc. under which no earmarking of funds to the special component plan is usually made. Under each of the remaining sectors 10 per cent to 40 per cent of the outlays are required to be provided for SCP so as to ensure adequate general sector flow of funds to special component plan. In order to ensure a higher percentage of outlay for SCP, divisible outlays in the different sectors are quantified and the percentage outlays to be set apart for SCP by each department is indicated to the departments at the time of formulation of plan proposals.

The district-wise allocations of the different sectoral outlays under SCP are worked out applying the prescribed formula as per Table 4.11.

Table 4.11
Criteria for District-wise Allocation of Funds for SCP

Sector	*Criteria*
IRDP & NREP	Existing norms which are laid down by the Government of India on the basis of small and marginal farmers and agricultural labourers.
Agriculture/Minor irrigation/soil conservation Command Area Development	No. of scheduled caste cultivators and scheduled caste beneficiaries of land reforms other than Kudikidappukar.
Land Reforms/Animal Husbandry/ Dairy Development	The number of Scheduled Caste agricultural labourers in each district.
Power/Roads/Medical and Public health/Water supply	No. of Scheduled Caste habitats identified in each district.
Community development/forest/ Village and small scale industries/ Housing/Social welfare/nutrition etc.	The Scheduled Caste population in the district.
Education & Training, Cooperation.	According to needs, based on the number of institutions.

Eighth Plan Perspectives

Based on the Seventh Plan performance the probable outlays for each district for the VIII Plan have been estimated. The tentative outlays for each district are worked out as per Table 4.12.

Table 4.12
Proposed District-wise Outlay During Eighth Plan

Name of District	Tentative Outlay for the VIII Five Year Plan	
	(Rs. lakhs) State plan	50% Central Assistance scheme
1. Trivandrum	106,20.00	20.08.00
2. Quilon	83,02.00	16,32.00
3. Pathanamthitta	61,12.00	9,18.00
4. Alleppey	82,57.00	10,91.00
5. Kottayam	80,17.00	10,08.00
6. Idukki	73,12.00	9,93.00
7. Ernakulam	91,20.00	16,98.00
8. Trichur	101,25.00	17,58.00
9. Palghat	90,00.00	19,46.00
10. Malappuram	84,75.00	13,91.00
11. Kozhikode	91,05.00	14,96.00
12. Wayanad	54,90.00	6,03.00
13. Cannanore	69,60.00	12,56.00
14. Kasaragod	56,05.00	7,81.00
Total	1,125,00.00	185,85.00

In addition to indicating the tentative outlay for each district, the criteria for allocation for different sectors are also made.

The DDC is required to allocate the indicated outlay among the three sub-committees taking into account the sectors coming under their purview. Each sub-committee in turn will apportion the outlays among the different urban area/panchayats/blocks in the district. The past allocations for different areas could be used as a guide in fixing the allocations. In the absence of specific details the following rule of thumb would be adopted for the distribution of outlays.

1. Population as the basis (say 50% of the total allocations)
2. Agricultural workers (say 15%)
3. SC/ST population (percentage outlay equivalent to their percentage in the total population)

4. For block level schemes equally to all blocks (say 10%)
5. For district level schemes (balance outlay)

MADHYA PRADESH

Untied Fund

There is no discretionary fund for district planning. At present, the aspects of minimum needs programmes are only approved at the district level. For the implementation of items pertaining to the Minimum Needs Programme which are implemented by different departments, the district share of these items are passed on to the district level. This amount is obtained from different departments and given to the district planning boards. The district planning boards are free to decide the location of these schemes. There is no fixed allocation for the implementation of these programmes, whatever amount the sectoral departments are prepared to part with is passed on to the planning board and thus there is no upper ceiling on the amount which can be given to the district planning boards. During the four years, each district was provided with Rs. 4 lakhs for the construction of roads, similarly from public health engineering department, 3 to 3.5 lakhs have been provided. As the education department is tied up with several ongoing schemes it is not in a position to spare amount for taking up construction of new schools. Moreover, due to recent drought conditions, there was shortage of fund and only a small percentage of the total allocation could be passed on to the district planning boards.

The total amount available for the implementation of MNP at the district level is distributed uniformly among the districts in the state. The district planning boards have to follow certain guidelines in selecting their schemes. In case of roads, they can propose only roads upto 5 km length. The alignment of proposed road has to be decided by the planning board, the amount spent on each scheme is also not fixed. It depends on the availability of total amount for that particular scheme. The number of units implemented and different schemes and their location has to be decided by the district planning board and there is no interference from above in this regard. The amount flowing to the district under MNP from different departments is spent only for the implementation of those schemes which belong to those departments. Thus, the amount available from PWD is spent only on construction of roads by the district planning board.

The exercise for identifying district sector schemes and district sector outlays are in progress. The heads of development departments have been required to provide districtwise break-up of programmes/schemes along with their financial allocations. Criterion of allocating funds to districts will be developed on the basis of the above study. At present the District Planning Boards and Panchayat Raj institutions plan and implement schemes.

MAHARASHTRA

Financial Allocation

As a prerequisite to introducing district level planning in the fifth five-year Plan the plan schemes of the state government were classified into (1) state level and (2) district level schemes. The intention was to devolve upon the DPDCs about 60 per cent of the plan outlay of the state government. With this in view, schemes like major irrigation were classified as district level schemes. Later on in 1976-77, on practical consideration these were reclassified as state level schemes. This brought down the proportion of district level schemes in the state plan.

In this state about 40 to 45 per cent of the total state plan outlays are earmarked for district level programmes to be planned at the district level. Out of this, the amount required for state pool schemes are retained and only the allocation for district level schemes are distributed among the districts. In 1983-84 out of the total district plan allocation of Rs. 646.65 crores state pool schemes amounted to Rs. 190.75 crores i.e. 29.5 per cent of the total entitlement of the district level schemes. Consequently the plan funds annually devolved upon the DPDCs were further reduced to about 30-32 per cent of plan expenditure.

While allocating its resources to various districts a formula has been adopted. This formula takes care of the basic objective of district planning namely removal of inter-district imbalance in levels of development. This formula is broadly as per Table 4.13.

As per the formula, agricultural backwardness is measured by the Geometric mean of value added from agriculture per hectare. Similarly, backwardness in communication is measured by the geometric mean of road and rail length per 100 sq. km. and per lakh population.

Table 4.13
Criteria for Allocation of Funds to Districts in Maharashtra

Item	Percentage to total allocation
1. Total population	60
2. Urban population	5
3. Backward class population	5
4. Backwardness in agriculture	5
5. Backwardness in irrigation	4
6. Industrial backwardness	5
7. Communications backwardness	5
8. Special problems on drought prone areas	3
9. Problems of the people in the coastal area	1.50
10. Problems in forest areas	1.50
11. Amount retained at the state level for solving special problems	5
Total	100

Thus the divisible plan outlay in the state is distributed amongst the districts according to this 11 components' formula, in proportion to the respective factor or indicator. Thus 60 per cent of the plan outlays to be distributed is allocated to the district in proportion to their population to the total population of the state. Five per cent is allocated in proportion to the urban population to the total urban population of the state and vice versa. As all the factors except population and urban population are indicators of backwardness the relatively under developed districts get larger allocations (Table 4.14).

The outlays of the state pool scheme are distributed between districts as required by the particular schemes and no formula is followed in this regard. As a result some districts get a larger share of the state pool scheme fund.

While calculating the financial ceiling for the districts the annual expenditure in the districts of all district level schemes including state pool schemes in the previous year is taken into account. Based on the annual expenditure, district allocations are worked out and any amount spent in excess is taken into consideration while working out the ceiling for subsequent year. It may be noted that only 30 per cent of the excess expenditure or shortage is adjusted while calculating the ceilings. Thus the adjustment calculated are only partially deviated in district allocations by these state pool schemes.

Table 4.14
District Plan Ceilings During 1988-89 in Maharashtra on the Basis of Formula of Weightages

(Rs. in crores)

Sl. No.	Name of Dist.	Population 60%	SC/ST (OBC population 5%)	Urban population 5%	Agriculture backwardness 5%	Communication backwardness 5%
1	2	3	4	5	6	7
1.	Gr. Bombay	35.91	1.37	9.49	-	
2.	Thane	13.67	1.84	1.73	0.84	1.48
3.	Raigad	7.64	0.53	0.24	0.51	0.62
4.	Ratnagiri	7.68	0.28	0.20	0.91	0.48
5.	Sindhudurg	4.33	0.16	0.11	0.52	0.27
6.	Nashik	14.33	2.14	1.06	1.33	0.97
7.	Dhule	9.97	1.93	0.45	1.17	0.99
8.	Jalgaon	11.93	0.81	0.81	0.87	0.89
9.	Pune	19.13	1.22	2.08	1.06	1.09
10.	Ahmednagar	14.41	1.30	0.48	1.39	1.09
11.	Satara	10.38	0.55	0.55	0.75	0.45
12.	Sangli	9.16	0.53	0.41	0.48	0.39
13.	Solapur	13.38	1.00	0.96	1.18	1.03
14.	Kolhapur	12.29	0.68	0.70	0.09	1.08
15.	Buldhana	7.66	0.60	0.05	1.25	0.84
16.	Akola	9.12	0.78	0.55	1.36	0.78
17.	Amravati	9.28	0.97	0.65	0.97	0.97
18.	Yeotmal	8.52	1.08	0.31	0.97	0.86
19.	Nagpur	11.56	0.98	1.68	0.74	1.45
20.	Wardha	4.82	0.36	0.32	0.59	0.46
21.	Bhandara	9.61	0.81	0.31	1.40	1.27
22.	Chandrapur	6.82	0.93	0.17	1.06	1.22
23.	Gadchiroli	3.06	0.42	0.07	0.47	0.56
24.	Aurangabad	7.36	0.49	0.32	0.83	0.99
25.	Jalna	4.72	0.32	0.21	0.53	0.63
26.	Beed	7.64	0.53	0.24	0.97	1.06
27.	Parbhani	8.99	0.77	0.35	1.05	0.97
28.	Nanded	8.39	0.91	0.40	0.77	0.97
29.	Osmanabad	5.02	0.43	0.16	0.53	0.62
30.	Latur	6.37	0.54	0.20	0.67	0.78
	Total	303.15	25.26	25.26	25.26	25.26

Irrigation backward-ness 5%	Industrial backward-ness 5%	Coastal Dist. 1.5%	Drought prone area 3%	Forest areas 1.5%	Total col. 1 to 12	Ceiling communi-cated to the Dist
8	9	10	11	12	13	14
-	-	-	-		46.77	47.00
0.65	-	2.51	-	0.50	23.22	23.00
0.39	0.37	1.93		0.19	12.42	12.50
0.49	1.28	2.01	-	0.02	13.35	13.50
0.27	0.71	1.13	-	0.01	7.51	8.00
0.86	0.65	-	1.83	0.45	23.62	23.50
0.48	1.50	-	1.12	0.50	18.11	18.00
0.25	1.47	-	0.75	0.26	18.04	18.00
0.13	-	-	1.25	0.12	26.08	26.00
-	0.09	-	2.43	0.21	21.40	21.50
1.06	0.62	-	0.92	0.14	15.42	15.50
0.82	1.18	-	1.08	0.03	14.08	14.00
0.92	0.74	-	2.18	0.02	21.41	21.50
0.25	0.09	-	-	0.22	15.40	15.00
1.30	1.19	-	0.25	0.12	13.26	13.50
1.16	1.24	-		0.10	15.09	15.00
1.49	1.32	-		0.50	16.15	16.00
1.44	0.42	-	-	0.44	15.04	15.00
0.97		-	-	0.29	17.67	17.50
0.53	0.59	-	-	0.10	7.77	8.00
-	1.53	-	-	0.50	15.43	15.50
0.17	0.79	-	-	1.69	12.85	12.50
0.07	0.36	-	-	0.76	5.77	6.00
1.26	1.22	-	0.81	0.06	13.34	14.00
0.81	0.78	-	0.53	0.03	8.56	9.50
1.18	1.32	-	1.18	0.02	14.14	13.50
0.27	1.48	-	-	0.03	14.64	13.00
0.27	1.48	-	-	0.14	13.33	13.50
0.84	0.86	-	0.36	0.05	8.87	9.00
1.06	1.09	-	0.47	0.08	11.26	11.50
20.23	25.26	7.58	15.16	7.58	480.00	480.00

Untied Funds

In the state there is a provision for special allocation at the rate of Rs. 2 crores for each district for taking up small works based on the felt needs of the district. The schemes include missing road links, class rooms in primary school, samaj mandirs etc. each such work costing not more than 3 lakhs to be completed in one working season. The Seventh Plan provision for these programmes is Rs. 320 crores. These programmes are finalised by the DPDC in accordance with the guidelines issued by the state government. These funds are over and above the normal district plan allocation made available to each DPDC. Necessary funding and other powers have been delegated to the district officers for ensuring speedy implementation of these programmes. For 1988-89 an amount of Rs. 64 crores has been recommended as untied fund.

Procedure for Release of Grants

(a) Immediately after the commencement of the financial year, the administrative departments are required to communicate directly to the officers responsible for implementing the schemes at the district level the grants placed at their disposal under intimation to the heads of departments instead of channelising the grants to the district officers through the head of departments. (b) The release relates to all individual programmes for which provisions have actually been made in the budget and vote on account has been carried out by the state legislature. The district-wise break up is strictly in accordance with provisions approved for each district and so included in the annual plan document. (c) Simultaneously the administrative departments are required to issue directly such formula and administrative sanctions in respect of individual schemes as may be necessary for audit purposes. (d) For issuing such administrative sanctions a period of one month following the vote of the demands by the state legislature is allowed. However, in case these orders are likely to be delayed for some reasons, heads of departments have been empowered to authorise the implementing officers at the district level to continue to implement the schemes included in the annual plan for the year upon a maximum period of three months pending receipt of formal orders from the administrative departments subject to the condition that the provision for the scheme/schemes is retained in the budget for the year.

The implementation of this procedure is closely watched at the state level by the planning department and at the district level by the

Collector and Member Secretary of the DPDC. The Collector's report to the planning department in instances of delay in respect of release orders as also sanctions and such instances are followed up with the concerned administrative departments by the officers of the planning department appointed to liaison with the DPDCs.

Power of Reappropriation

As a sequel to the policy of district planning, it is necessary to ensure that the outlays earmarked for each district in accordance with the formula of weightages are utilised within the district during the year. In the implementation of various programmes situations arise when additional funds are required for certain programmes. While there could be savings under some other programmes in the normal course, the reappropriation of savings would be done by the heads of departments and controlling officers with reference to the total amount available under a particular major head of account controlled by these officers. As a result this freedom enjoyed by the head of department and controlling officers, the savings from one district could be diverted to others resulting in variations in the district plan outlays at the end of the year. Government, has, therefore, vested the powers of reappropriation of savings in the DPDCs subject to certain conditions. Orders relating to the powers of the DPDCs in regard to reappropriation within the approved annual plan have been issued. The Heads of departments are required to take into account such reappropriations while formulating the revised estimates pertaining to the grants controlled by them. Out of the eight meetings generally held for DPDC one meeting is exclusively reserved for reappropriation before 31st December. DPDC can suggest reappropriation from one department to other and one scheme to other before reappropriation suggestions for additional amount or reduction of amount with justification are invited from the implementing officers. Generally five per cent of the amount is reappropriated every year.

ORISSA

Untied Funds

In January, 1986 the State Government issued instructions to all the Collectors regarding the utilisation of untied funds. These funds are placed at the disposal of the district planning committee, for taking up small but essential development works which cannot be accommodated within the district sectoral plans. The DPCs are required to formulate important programmes/schemes to fill up some essential gaps in the district and to meet some immediate needs of the people of the area. Since the amount is not tied to any sector the DPCs are given full freedom in the choice of the programmes/schemes of local importance. For 1988-89 an outlay of Rs. 750 lakhs has been recommended as untied fund.

The untied fund available in Puri district during 1985-86 was Rs. 8.44 lakhs which increased to Rs. 17.82 lakhs in 1986-87 and in 1987-88 it was Rs. 27.48 lakhs. Out of Rs. 17.82 lakhs made available during 1986-87, 75 schemes/projects were financed. For the utilisation of the untied funds proposals are received from the Chairmen of different working groups as well as from members of DPC.

Even untied funds in this state is being distributed among different districts on the basis of the following formula. (1) Population .... 50 per cent (2) Backwardness (measured on the basis of certain infrastructure facilities' availability ... 50 per cent).

As the districts have not been provided with their share of finance from the total plan fund of the state this is the only amount available to them on the basis of it they can implement schemes of their choice and need. Thus the district officers have the freedom of planning and execution of schemes at the district level only to the extent of this limited amount of untied funds.

UTTAR PRADESH

Financial Allocation

In this state there is clearcut demarcation of fund for state and district level schemes. 30 per cent of the total plan outlay has been earmarked for district sector schemes and the rest (70 per cent) has been set apart for the state sector schemes. However, the share of outlay for the district sector schemes has been steadily decreasing from year to year and during 1987-88 it was only 23.90 per cent of the total plan outlay. Thus it has never been possible to allocate 30 per cent of the total fund of the state plan for the district level schemes. However, in the hilly districts of Uttar Pradesh the share of district sector schemes are as high as 50 per cent (Table 4.15). Out of this 50 per cent entire share of the district sector is allocated in the hilly region whereas in the plain districts only 90 per cent of the state sector schemes is given to the districts. Out of the remaining, 5 per cent of the funds of district sector schemes two per cent of this is again given to the district on the basis of their performance in generating national saving. Similarly three per cent of the total district sector scheme is kept as reserve with the state for the purpose of special requirements.

In case of tribal districts some of the schemes identified in the district sector in the plains are placed in the state sector in the hills. Thus there is some difference in the pattern of allocation and the classification of state and district sector schemes in operation in this state.

Table 4.15

Outlay Allocated to District Sector in U.P.

(Rs. in crores)

Year	*Total Plan outlay*	*Outlay for district sector*	*District sector as % of total plan outlay*
Plains			
1982-83	1082.00	282.56	26.11
1983-84	1235.00	339.03	27.45
1984-85	1436.00	349.13	24.31
1985-86	1573.00	385.00	24.70
1986-87	1945.00	441.57	22.70
1987-88	2165.00	517.50	23.90
Hill Region			
1982-83	120.00	63.01	52.50
1983-84	140.00	73.13	52.23
1984-85	165.00	87.25	52.87
1985-86	177.00	94.52	53.40
1986-87	205.00	106.73	52.06
1987-88	235.00	118.67	50.50
Plains & Hill			
1982-83	1202.00	345.57	28.74
1983-84	1375.00	412.16	29.97
1984-85	1601.00	436.38	27.25
1985-86	1750.00	479.52	27.40
1986-87	2150.00	548.30	25.50
1987-88	2400.00	636.17	26.51

The divisible district sector outlay is being distributed among various districts of the state based on the following formula. (Table 4.16) and (Table 4.17).

Table 4.16

Indicators for Distribution of Expenditure on District Plan in Plains

	Indicator		*% weight*
1.	Total population		50
2.	Scheduled caste/tribe population		5
3.	Marginal and landless labourers		10
4.	Backwardness		
	i.	agriculture	5
	ii.	industry	5
	iii.	roads	5
	iv.	village electrification	5
	v.	no beds in hospital	5
	vi.	problem villages for drinking water	5
			95
5.	Reserved for special programmes		5
			100

Table 4.17

Indicators for Distribution of Expenditure on District Plan in Hill Areas

	Indicator	*% weight*
1.	Population	50
2.	SC/ST population	5
3.	Marginal farmers & landless labourers	10
4.	Backwardness in agriculture production	5
5.	Industrial backwardness	5
6.	Backwardness in rural electrification	5
7.	Backwardness in beds in hospital	5
8.	Problem villages for drinking water	5
9.	Geographical area	5
10.	Effective forest	5
		100

The indicators of backwardness have been worked out as per the details given below:

(1) Agricultural backwardness-ratio of net cropped area and gross value of agricultural output per net hectare.

(2) Industrial backwardness-population of each district was divided by per capita industrial output and the values so obtained were added up. The values of each district were expressed as percentage of the total for the state.

(3) Roads: Geographical area of each district divided by the total road mileage.

(4) Village electrification : Percentage of electrified villages to the total number of villages.

(5) Medical facilities: No. of beds in allopathic hospitals.

(6) Drinking water : Percentage of scarcity villages to total villages.

Re-appropriation

The heads of the departments do not have the power of reappropriation of funds at their level. All the reappropriation proposals regarding district sector are to come from the DPMC and are approved at the state level. The reappropriation is made at the state level according to these approved proposals. While doing so it is assured that in no case funds of one district are diverted to the other districts.

WEST BENGAL

Allocation of Fund

Special Fund

Besides the normal allocation for different departments or authorities a separate budget has been introduced in the state with effect from 1985-86 as district plan schemes. Funds from this budget head have been placed at the disposal of the district planning authorities. The district authorities are supposed to utilise these funds to meet the critical gap between the fund required for implementing the district plan and the actual availability. For 1987-88, Rs. 24 crores were provided. For 1988-89 the amount available under this district scheme is Rs. 24.00 crores. Thus allocation is utilised mainly for distribution of mini kits, provision

Table 4.18
Provisional Annual Plan (Budget) of Midnapor District in West Bengal for the Year 1987-88 Showing Sources of Fund

(Rs. in lakhs)

Sl. No.	Name of Sector	Total	NREP	RLEGP	IRDP
1	2	3	4	5	6
1.	Agriculture including soil conservation & agricultural marketing	3569.925	85.00	113.30	182.75
2.	Minor irrigation	2322.67	100.00	235.00	89.00
3.	Irrigation & waterways	422.00	-	-	-
4.	Animal husbandry	453.17	-	-	78.70
5.	Veterinary services	27.35	-	-	-
6.	Fisheries	670.715	-	114.00	19.86
7.	C & SSI including sericulture, handloom, biogas etc.	5101.14	-	-	251.00
8.	Forests	344.21	120.94	-	-
9.	Roads	638.42	172.60	237.63	-
10.	Cooperation	81.40	-	-	-
11.	Education including Primary + second. + social education & library	2118.40	37.00	13.00	-
12.	Youth services & sports	19.87	-	-	-
13.	Rural electrification	687.97	-	-	-
14.	Special programme for tribes (article 275 + VIII finance commission)	81.00	-	-	-
15.	Health & family welfare (excluding central programme)	155.43	-	-	-
16.	Panchayat	6.76	-	-	-
17.	Community development	9.508	-	-	-
18.	Public Health (PHE + rural sanitation)	657.60	28.30	10.50	-
19.	Local Govt. (municipality)	39.44	-	-	-
20.	Tourism	1.50	-	-	-
21.	Social welfare	116.17	-	-	-
22.	P.W.D. & construction board	25.75	-	-	-
23.	Digha Dev. scheme	21.00	-	-	-
24.	Rural Housing other than C.D.	129.57	-	119 27	-
25.	Housing (rental & loan)	2.00	-	-	-
		17703.469	543.84	842.70	621.31

CSMI	DEPTT	Flow to SCP	Flow TSP	SCA for SC	SCA for ST
7	8	9	10	11	12
-	326.586	48.98	26.12	79.50	52.50
189.00	433.12	64.96	34.65	58.00	77.00
-	410.00	61.50	32.80	-	
-	42.82	6.42	3.42	9.00	19.00
-	26.35	3.95	2.10	-	-
-	113.845	17.07	9.10		-
	890.58	133.58	71.24	20.00	21.00
-	136.67	20.50	10.93	7.00	14.00
-	165.19	24.77	13.21	2.00	21.00
	81.40	12.21	6.51	-	-
-	1446.00	216.90	115.68	364.95	238.85
-	18.87	2.83	1.50	-	-
-	687.97	103.19	55.03	-	-
-	-	-	-	-	-
-	155.43	23.31	12.43	-	-
-	6.76	1.01	0.54	-	-
-	9.508	1.42	0.76	-	-
-	532.50	79.87	42.60	4.00	3.50
-	39.44	5.91	3.15		-
-	1.50	-		-	-
-	115.17	17.27	9.21	-	-
-	10.00	1.50	0.80	-	-
-	15.75	2.36	1.26		-
-	-	-		3.00	2.00
-	2.00	-	-	-	-
189.0	5667.46	849.46	453.04	547.45	448.85

of minor irrigation and drainage facilities, protection of embankments, construction of godowns, storage facilities, construction of rural roads, small bridges and culverts, primary school buildings, huts for scheduled tribe people etc. The funds are provided to the implementing agencies at the district. Schemes which are relatively small and are of non-technical nature like that implemented under NREP, RLEGP etc. and are worth Rs. 50,000 or below are taken up by the Gram panchayats. Other schemes having an estimated value of more than Rs. 50,000 fall under the jurisdiction of the panchayat samithi. Other schemes which fall under the category of minimum needs programme like upgradation of primary school, construction of rural health sub-centres etc. are entrusted to Z.P. According to this distribution of work the finance is also distributed among the Z.P. panchayat samithies and Gram panchayat under intimation to the district planning committee.

For other programmes, fund is released under various budget heads by the respective departments to their district level officers endorsing copies of allotment to the district planning committee (Table 4.18). As mentioned earlier the district level officers in turn redistribute the fund among the block planning committees on priority basis for block level schemes. However, they retain a portion of it for execution of district level and inter block schemes. The fund allotted under district plan schemes to the district is retained by the DPC and is distributed among various agencies for meeting their critical gap, when necessary.

Most of the states in the country have set aside a part of divisible fund for schemes at district and below at an average of about 30 to 40 per cent of the state plan allocation. Out of these allocations about 80 per cent is generally reserved for the schemes which have been formulated keeping in view the guidelines given by the state level departments and approved by the state planning departments. In most cases sector-wise allocation of the district fund is communicated by the state planning department leaving little scope for the district level planning body to propose schemes and fix up its priority based on the local potentialities, problems and need of the people. However, in some states to provide some freedom to the district planning bodies a very small percentage of allocation was set aside for implementing such schemes which the authorities feel are important and useful for their region. These were generally very small schemes. Atleast to this extent the district planning bodies had freedom of selecting and implementing schemes without any interference from the state level. This amount is symbolic to devolution of financial power for local level planning. To make micro level planning a success it will be necessary to empower the local level agencies to have the full freedom to plan and implement at the local level for the entire district. As a major share of the district level allocation is not at present in the hands of these agencies it requires much more effort for real decentralisation of the financial powers.

Notes and References

1. Lakshminarayana, S., op. cit., p. 7.
2. Barua, Bhaskar, p. 2.
3. Ibid.
4. Govt. of Gujarat, Review of Sixth Five Year Plan (1980-85) Planning Division, General Administration Dept., June 1986, p. 361.
5. Ibid., p. 361.
6. Govt. of Gujarat, op. cit., p. 361.
7. Kumar Ajit, op. cit., p. 5.

V

Plan Formulation, Implementation and Monitoring

In an ideal situation the micro level plans should be prepared by a team well conversant with the area and having technical expertise, in consultation with the people. But the current practice in different states in the country is to formulate micro level plans for districts, sub-divisions, blocks even mandals at the district level. The plan proposals are prepared by the sectoral officers within the financial ceiling and the guidelines indicated to them from the state headquarters. The proposals are approved at the district as well as state level with certain modifications. As regards implementation of these schemes, it is invariably undertaken by the district level departments and below. The monitoring and review of implementation of plan is generally done in the meetings held at the district level and at these meetings efforts are made for coordination among different departmental schemes.

The practice prevalent in different states in respect of plan formulation, implementation and monitoring are discussed below.

ANDHRA PRADESH

Plan Formulation

In the state of Andhra Pradesh the sectoral plans as part of the Annual Action Plan of the districts are formulated at the state as well as district level. The Heads of the departments of agriculture, sericulture, animal husbandry etc. formulate plan for their sector at the state level.[1] For other sectors the plans are prepared by the concerned district Heads of Departments and approved by the District Planning Board. These plans are dovetailed into state sectoral plans after a series of meetings between the Heads of Departments and the state planning departments. The sector-wise district segments are consolidated by the state planning department and communicated to the District Collector for follow up and monitoring at the district level.

Different agencies such as DRDA, SC/BC/ST/Housing Corporation etc. prepare their Annual Action Plans taking into account the resource flow from Centre/State and institutional finance. Similarly the Lead Bank officer is responsible for the preparation of the District Credit Plan. The district plans of these district level corporations and agencies are not integrated into the District Annual Plan.[2]

The district level officers and the field staff are the main instruments of the programme implementation. While executing the programmes, they follow the guidelines of the respective departments. Some of the programmes of the line departments are directly implemented by their departmental staff, whereas the beneficiary oriented programmes are implemented through the Mandal Praja Parishads. Thus, the programmes of DRDA, SC Service Cooperative Finance Corporation, ST Finance Corporation, ITDA, District level committee on women welfare, weaker sections housing corporation, society for training and employment programme (STEP), Handicapped welfare corporation, Minorities corporation, Dairy development corporation (District level), Forest Development corporation and Zilla Parishads implement their programmes through Mandal Praja Parishad.

Monitoring of the District Plans

Monitoring of the implementation of all the development schemes (both plan and non-plan) including those implemented by local bodies, corporate bodies like District Rural Development Agency (DRDA), Integrated Tribal Development Agency (ITDA) Andhra Pradesh State Electricity Board (APSEB), Agricultural Market Committee, Drainage Board etc. is done by the District Development and Review Board. These Boards also review the implementation of priority programmes like 20-point programme, Crucial balancing and incentive programmes viz., 'Pragathi Patham', 'Telugu Grameena Kranthi Patham' and also the functioning of all the regulatory agencies and departments like civil supplies, excise etc.

ASSAM

Planning Process

In this state, even though sub-divisions have been recognised as the unit for planning, the plan formulation exercise is carried out at the district level by the sectoral heads. The exercise commences by 1st of April when the planning and development department at the state level communicates to the Deputy Commissioner the quantum of fund likely to be available for the sub-division during the year. In turn, the Deputy Commissioner informs the district Heads of the Departments the tentative allocation to the respective departments in the sub-division. Accordingly the draft plan for the sub-division is prepared by the sectoral heads at this level. They identify schemes and projects for sub-divisions keeping in view the local needs on the one hand and potentialities on the other. The draft plan thus formulated is then submitted to the Deputy Commissioner by 31st May.

These draft sectoral plans are scrutinised by the core group at the district level and finalises in consultation with the district level sectoral heads. Then it is placed before the sub-divisional planning and development council for approval. Selection of sites, fixation of priorities, targets for different sectors are also decided at this level.

In the meanwhile the state plan outlay is finalised by the Planning Commission making it possible to work out the sectoral outlay for each sub-division and communicated to the Dy. Commissioner. This facilitates finalisation of projects/operational plan for different sectors as per the availability of fund, by the Heads of Development departments. While doing so they also keep in view the priorities fixed by the Sub-Divisional Planning and Development Council.

It may be noted that the on-going schemes and activities under various sectors are given first priority. This is followed by expansion proposals of on-going activities. New schemes and proposals are taken up to the extent the fund permits.[1] The operational plan is supposed to contain the details of each project regarding inputs, outputs, physical targets fixed, location, number of beneficiaries targetted etc. This operational plan is then submitted to the Deputy Commissioner who places it before the core group for scrutiny and revision (if necessary) and then the operational plan is considered by the sub-divisional planning and development council for approval.

The Deputy Commissioners are required to forward the operational plan of the sub-divisions as approved by the sub-divisional planning and development councils in specific proforma to the respective Heads of Department. Copy of these plans are also marked to the administrative departments concerned for sanction, and the Planning and Development Department for information and follow-up.

Implementation and Monitoring

The operational Annual Action Plan for the sub-divisions is implemented by the district Heads of Development Departments as per the guidelines and directions received from the state headquarters. The progress of implementation of these schemes is monitored by the Deputy Commissioner through the District Development Committee meetings which are held in the first week of each month. The Deputy Commissioner chairs these meetings and in these committee meetings reviews of implementation of plan schemes are made and inter-departmental coordination is effected.

Generally the decisions taken in these meetings are complied with by all the district level Heads of Departments. At the same time in case of any difficulty the matter can be referred to the Planning and Development Department at the state level.

The sub-Divisional Planning and Development Council is also required to monitor the progress of implementation of sub-divisional plan atleast twice a year.

At the state level also review meetings are held on quarterly basis but additional meetings are also held as and when review of a particular sector is found necessary. These meetings are conducted by the Special Commissioner of the Planning and Development Department wherein all the Secretaries and Heads of Development Departments are represented and even Chief Minister occasionally chairs such review meetings. In these meetings, besides reviewing the progress of implementation of sectoral programmes, inter-departmental problems are also sorted out.

BIHAR

Planning Process

In Bihar Officials as well as non-officials are associated with plan formulation exercise which commences in the month of August/ September. Thus proposals for respective sectors to be included in the draft plan are invited from all the sectoral heads. At the same time all MLAs, MPs, Block Pramukh and BDO are requested to identify the schemes based on the need of the area and submit their proposals within a month to the District Planning Cell. The District planning officer, on receipt of the draft plan from the sectoral heads and the suggestions from the people's representatives compiles the proposals keeping in view the guidelines/instructions given by the Government. This compiled plan is then submitted to the District Magistrate who in turn fixes up the priority of different schemes. These proposals are then placed before the executive committee for DPDC for technical examination and integration. In the meeting of the DPDC these proposals are discussed and approved with some additions and omissions as necessary. These draft plans are then forwarded to the state government for its final approval.

Monitoring

The progress of the implementation of the Annual Action plan is discussed in the monthly meetings of the DPDC. The departments are also required to furnish their monthly report indicating (1) title of the scheme; (2) unit of the physical target; (3) estimated cost; (4) allotment available with the agency; (5) expenditure incurred; (6) current physical progress, along with their remarks.

GUJARAT

Plan Formulation

The Government of Gujarat during the course of implementation of their plan programmes, realised the need for quick decision making and freedom for selecting schemes/works of local importance at the local level particularly for the Minimum Needs or missing links in difficult and remote areas. Moreover, to get the people involved in planning process at micro level, it was considered necessary to extend the idea of decentralisation of planning process. Consequently, in 1979, a suggestion was putforth by the State Planning Board to actively involve the District Planning Boards in the process of formulation of Annual

Plans.[4] Since 1980-81 this has been operationalised and the District Planning Boards formulate schemes keeping in view the specific local needs to be implemented with the discretionary and incentive outlays provided to them. In this task the DPDC is assisted by the Taluka Planning Committees. Thus the District Planning Board conveys the likely allotment of discretionary and incentive outlays to taluka planning committees well in advance. Taluka Planning committees are expected to formulate the proposals within the indicated financial ceiling and suggest their priorities on the basis of the need of the villages. The District Planning Board finalises the proposals received from the Taluka Planning Committees on the basis of the guidelines issued by State Government.

Over and above the discretionary and incentive outlays which are exclusively put at their disposal, the District Planning Boards also formulate proposals for 80% of normal district level schemes. The DPBs collect proposals from the concerned District officers for sectoral schemes and from the district panchayats for panchayat sector schemes, prepared against the ceilings indicated to them in advance. These annual plan proposals are formulated keeping in view the priorities and guidelines indicated by the State Government. These proposals contain suggestions for adequate allocations for specific schemes, inclusion of new schemes or deletion of on-going schemes etc. These proposals are discussed in the executive planning committees of the DPBs and on finalisation approved by the DPB. The approved sectoral plans are returned to the concerned departments and a set of these plans (compiled district plan) is submitted to the state planning department while finalising the state plan, the district proposals are kept in view. In case the proposals included in the district plan are not acceptable to the Heads of the Departments they are required to communicate the details with reasons of exclusion to the concerned DPBs.

An attempt is made during the Seventh Plan to refine the exercise of plan formulation at the district level. This has been done through organising workshops on plan formulation in all the districts by the District Planning Boards.[5] These workshops were attended by all the members of the DPBs which include MPs, MLAs, President of District Panchayat, President of Social Justice Committee of the District Panchayat etc. Moreover, representatives of academic institutions, knowledgeable non-officials and representatives of the industries in the district were also invited. Representatives from sectoral departments at the state level and all the district level officers also participate in these workshops.

In these workshops the District Plans prepared in the routine manner were discussed. Keeping in view the resource potentials, local needs, inter-block imbalances and the state and national approach to the seventh plan, suggestions were made by the working groups of this workshop for modifying the district plan. These suggestions were taken care of by the Steering Committee formed at the district level while revising the district plan and forwarded to the steering groups charged with the responsibility of preparing state plan.

At state level, the Secretary (Planning) holds discussion sessions with the sectoral departments to ensure that the recommendations of the district are adequately reflected in the steering group reports.

Time Schedule

The Government of Gujarat, with a view to streamlining the process of formulation of scheme/works to be taken up out of discretionary and incentive outlay and their implementation has suggested a time schedule to be followed by DPBs. (Table 5.1).

In order to facilitate the task of plan formulation the District Planning Boards have also been supplied with the computerised information on 77 basic village amenities for the villages falling in their district.[6] The information on village amenities is being updated every year as on 1st October.

Monitoring

The plan implementation is monitored at different levels by different agencies. The District Planning Boards are entrusted with the responsibility of monitoring of 'Minimum Needs Programme' as well as family oriented programmes for poverty alleviation in the district. The Executive Planning Committee of the DPB meets every month to monitor the implementation of the schemes sanctioned by the DPB. In addition District Planning officers inspect the Projects financed by District Planning Board for expediting implementation and investigating complaints.

HIMACHAL PRADESH

Planning Process

Although the district planning and development committee and a planning cell are in existence in the districts of Himachal Pradesh, the exercise of plan formulation is still in the hands of the Heads of the Departments at the state level. The plan formulation starts with the issue of instructions by the state planning department to all the Heads of Departments concerned with plan schemes to formulate draft Annual Plan within the ceiling imposed. The sectoral Heads in turn get information and proposals from the district level officers as they are instrumental for the implementation of the schemes of local importance as well as those having inter-district coverage. On the basis of these suggestions, the sectoral heads formulate the sectoral plan for the state as a whole within the financial ceiling and forward to the State Planning Department. The state planning department consolidates these sectoral plan and presents the same to the State Planning Board.

The Chief Minister of the state also holds discussions with MLAs of each district separately, who indicate their views on the sectoral priorities and suggest better ways of managing their resources. These views are incorporated in the plan document in terms of broad sectoral priorities.

Table 5.1

Time Schedule for Plan Formulation—Gujarat State

	Particular	*Last date of compliance*
1.	To work out sector/subsectorwise allocation out of discretionary and incentive outlay for the year 1987-88.	30th November
2.	To inform taluka planning committees about talukawise tentative allocation of discretionary and incentive outlay.	30th November
3.	To obtain proposals from taluka Planning committees, implementing officers/institutions.	15th January
4.	To prepare note co-ordinating the sectorwise allocations and final proposals and get it approved by Executive committee.	31st January
5.	To get the approval of district planning board in principle for Annual Plan 1987-88.	25th February
6.	To inform concerned implementing officers regarding sanctions.	28th February
7.	To complete the preparation of schemes/works by implementing officers and intimate the same to Collector.	31st March

Plan Implementation and Monitoring

For implementation of plan schemes, the State Government has fixed norms for utilisation of funds under plan schemes for each quarter of the financial year. The norms fixed for each quarter is as under:

1. First quarter	20%
2. 2nd quarter	25%
3. 3rd quarter	30%
4. 4th quarter	25%

The progress reports in terms of financial, and physical content under plan schemes are reviewed in the quarterly meetings of District Planning and Development committee under the chairmanship of Minister/Deputy Commissioner of the district. All the Heads of the district offices participate in the meeting. The shortfalls, if any, are communicated to the concerned Heads of the Departments for initiating suitable measures to remove these shortfalls in the succeeding quarter. Subsequently the quarterly monitoring meetings at state level are also held under the chairmanship of Chief Secretary of the state. All the concerned Secretaries to the Government and Heads of the Department participate in the meeting. The financial and physical progress as per norms fixed by the Government, is reviewed in these meetings and heads of the department concerned are asked to make up their deficiency, if any, during the next quarter of the financial year.

JAMMU AND KASHMIR

Planning Process

The state of Jammu and Kashmir has adopted block as the primary unit of planning in the state. But till such time as machinery for formulating the block plan comes into existence, this task has been entrusted to the district level planning machinery. With the induction of block level planning total state plan, now consists of three parts (1) the state level plan, (2) the district level plan, and (3) the block level plan. Detailed guidelines have been issued by the government regarding the formulation of these plans.

In this state, the sectoral priorities are arrived at the state level after discussion with the Planning Commission. Accordingly, sectoral outlays for each district are arrived at.[7] The State Planning Department communicates these sectoral allocations and total outlay for the district plan as well as broad priorities and guidelines. Keeping in view this, a detailed district plan is drawn up by the district administration in consultation with the concerned heads of the departments at the district level. This state also has the perspective plans prepared for most of the districts through consultants which are also kept in view at the time of formulating the district plan.

Since 1986-87 lumpsum outlays for five broad sectors of economy are being communicated to the district authorities on the basis of which district development boards apportion the outlays for each of the sectors and sub-sectors after taking into consideration needs, priorities and guidelines issued by the Planning Department etc. These five broad sectors are as under:[8]

1. Agriculture and rural development
2. Industry and commerce
3. Power
4. Transport and communications, and
5. Social and community services.

The plan is then placed before the district development board where the location and operational aspects of various schemes are discussed and approved for implementation with suggested modifications if any. The strategy for implementation of the schemes is also discussed in detail in this forum and the action programme of each implementing department for the year is chalked out.

Review by State Cabinet

A unique feature in Jammu and Kashmir in respect of the micro level plan is that the review of implementation of Annual plan is done by the state cabinet. The entire cabinet participates in a meeting with the DDB at the district headquarters or at any other place in the district to review the plan progress. Senior officers of the government including heads of the departments also participate in these meetings. The members of the board are free to comment on the performance of the various departments.

Such problems which may require immediate attention of the cabinet are resolved on the spot.

KARNATAKA

Planning Process

Karnataka is one of the states where district authority have been empowered to plan for district sector schemes and execute it at their own, and the state level planning department or the Directors of different departments do not have a say in the plan prepared for the district.

The total amount earmarked for the district sector schemes are communicated to the Zilla Parishad and the different departments at the district level and are required to submit their plan proposals for the coming year. Generally this exercise at the district level starts in the month of February. While formulating the development plan priority is to be accorded to the on going schemes. There is not much freedom to select new schemes as per the choice and requirement due to availability of limited fund for this purpose. These proposals are forwarded to the planning unit. In this unit the plans are examined in terms of the economic viability of schemes and also compares the size of the scheme with the allocation for the sector. The planning unit places these compiled sectoral proposals before the District Planning and Development committee where plan of each sector is discussed with the departmental officers and suggestions are made. The sectoral officers are required to revise the plans in the light of the suggestions made by the DPDC and resubmit for its approval. The plan once approved by the committee is placed before the Zilla Parishad consisting of 65 members. The approved plan is sent to the Government by September. The Government approval is received by the district by the first week of April.

One important feature of micro planning in the state is that districts are required to give scheme-wise monthly break-up of physical and financial targets for the approved district plan and adhere to it strictly.

Plan Implementation and Monitoring

A plan approved by the Zilla Parishad is taken up for implementation by the sectoral officers at the district level with the help of mandal level officers. All the activities of the Zilla Parishad are implemented through nine standing committees mentioned earlier.

Monitoring and review of the development activities taken up by different departments and mandals are also done by the planning unit.

This unit receives the returns from the departments as well as mandals, by 10th of every month. These progress reports are placed before the Zilla Parishad which meets every month to review the progress.

KERALA

Planning Process

In Kerala, the planning exercise has been decentralised to the district level for the schemes meant for the development of scheduled caste. In order to facilitate planning for these schemes a habitat survey was carried out in 1982 in each district to identify SC habitats with 10 or more households clustered in an area. 4000 such habitats were identified. Basic data on items like available infrastructure facilities, occupational characteristics, educational qualification of SC population etc. were collècted. Based on these information and also discussions held with local knowledgeable persons, package of family-oriented schemes were identified. Along with the family oriented schemes area development programmes were also chalked out. This approach enabled preparation of a medium term development plan for the development of the area as well as scheduled caste families. This medium term plan is being used as a Master Plan document for identifying schemes for the annual plan.[9]

In each district, a working group has been constituted with the District Collector as Chairman and the district level officers as members. Once the Annual Plan allocations for special component plan to the districts are known, the Working Group calls for proposals from each district officer. While formulating proposals the departments have to adhere to the following guidelines:[10]

(a) First priority has to be given to spill over schemes. Schemes for which administrative clearance had already been given in the previous year will alone be considered.

(b) A critical assessment of all the ongoing schemes will be made so as to select those which could be continued.

(c) In proposing new schemes as far as possible composite schemes involving the coordinated efforts of more than one department will be given preference.

(d) Schemes will be prepared taking into account the suggestions in the comprehensive development plan for scheduled castes already prepared for each district. A mix of beneficiary oriented infrastructure and skill development programmes will be planned for the areas of scheduled caste concentration.

The plan proposals so formulated are discussed in detail in the working group. It is the responsibility of working group to ensure that each scheme is properly coordinated with the rest of the plan. Habitat level and family level coordination are properly worked out. In respect of economic development schemes the number of families proposed to be assisted in each habitat, package of schemes proposed for the different occupational groups, the expected additional income that would accrue to the assisted families, the number of families to be lifted above the poverty line under different programmes etc. are included in the proposals. For infrastructure development schemes, the Scheduled Caste Habitats where different departments have to concentrate their efforts are identified first and the programmes are drawn up accordingly. All the above programmes put together form the District Development Plan for scheduled castes. The District Annual Plan is placed before the District Advisory Committee for scheduled castes for advice before it is finalised.

In respect of all other schemes, the plans are formulated by the concerned departmental heads at the district level under the guidance of the state level heads of departments. The plan outlay is given in the budget under the concerned departments and the heads of departments have the power for reappropriation.

Implementation and Monitoring

The responsibility for implementation of the schemes included in the District Plan rests with the departments concerned. But the responsibility for achieving the targets in respect of the different departments rests with the District Collector assisted by the working groups and the departments.

In respect of SCP the District Advisory committee for Scheduled Castes and the District Development Council also review the implementation. The technical sanction for these schemes are given by the concerned district officer and the administrative sanction is accorded by the District Collector. The working groups are authorised to sanction SCP schemes upto Rs. 10 lakhs. For other schemes of different departments technical sanction is accorded by the respective departments, the coordination is effected in the District Development Council. Both the DDC and the Heads of departments review the progress.

MADHYA PRADESH

Planning and Implementation

In the state of Madhya Pradesh, presently the District Planning Boards and Panchayati Raj institutions are involved in planning and implementation of schemes pertaining to Minimum Needs Programme within the allotments placed by the heads of development departments to their district level organisations.[11]

A part of the budgetted outlay for construction of rural roads, construction of primary school buildings and construction of tubewells/ handpumps for providing drinking water facilities in problem villages under MNP is placed at the disposal of District Planning Boards. The planning and implementation of schemes/works within the allotment are carried out by the District Planning Boards through departmental agencies. Generally the District Planning Boards receive the proposals from the departments by July-August. In the meeting of the District Planning Board the proposals pertaining to these schemes are discussed and finalised. The District Planning Boards do not have any formal plan but only proceedings of their meetings. These proceedings are forwarded to the state planning board. In case of any suggestion on these proceedings by the State Planning Board it is again discussed at the District Planning Board. From the month of September-October implementation of these schemes will be taken up by the concerned departments.

The exercise for identifying district sector schemes, and district sector outlays is undertaken by both the state Planning Board and the Finance Department. The heads of development departments have been required to provide districtwise breakup of programmes/schemes along with their financial allocations. Criteria of allocating funds to districts will be developed after the above study is completed.

Plan Implementation and Monitoring

Different schemes of MNP planned at the district level are implemented by the concerned sectoral departments. With the Panchayati raj institutions made functional in the state, the implementation of certain schemes related to agriculture, forestry, veterinary and animal husbandry, public works, public health engineering, education, social welfare and cooperation have been given to the Janpad Panchayats (block level panchayats).

The district level Monitoring committee regularly monitors the implementation of plan programmes of the following sectors:

1. (a) Irrigation	ongoing major and medium irrigation works
(b) Minor Irrigation	ongoing minor and micro minor irrigation works of both irrigation and agricultural departments.
2. Public Health Engineering	Rural water supply schemes.
3. Public works department	Rural roads and buildings.
4. Rural Development	Poverty alleviation programmes.

The committee meets on a quarterly basis under the chairmanship of the Minister-in-charge of the district. The District Collector is its convenor. The District Planning Officer and his office provides secretarial assistance. The district level monitoring system is linked vertically with the State Planning Board/Planning Department where action is taken to help remove financial and organisational constraints in the implementation of plan programmes, if any.

MAHARASHTRA

Process of Plan Formulation

In Maharashtra unlike in many other states, plans for all the sectors for district level schemes are formulated by the departments at the district level, keeping in view the guidelines suggested by the State Planning Department. In the month of September the planning department of the state communicates to each district planning and development council (DPDC) the tentative financial ceiling within which the draft district annual plan is to be formulated by the DPDC. General guidelines as well as sectoral guidelines highlighting the policies and programmes contemplated at the state level and special requirements to be taken into consideration by the DPDC in formulating their draft district annual plans are also issued. Copies of these guidelines are also endorsed to various heads of departments and Secretariat departments. In turn they indicate to the DPDC the programmes which need to be considered while formulating the Draft District Annual plans.

The Collector and Member-Secretary through district planning officer issues circular to the district officers for submission of Annual Plan to DPDC.

The tentative allocation indicated to the district is simultaneously divided into different sectors taking into consideration previous three years' expenditure. This task is carried out by a small committee consisting of two to three MLAs, Collector, Chief Executive Officer and President of Zilla Parishad.

In the month of October the Collector and Member-Secretary then receive detailed proposals from the departments. These proposals are broadly classified into three categories viz., (1) continuing schemes or activities, (2) inevitable expansion, and (3) new programmes.

The proposals received from the Departments are then consolidated by the District Planning officer, which takes about 15 days. While consolidating the proposals the district planning officer is required to match the allocations within the proposed schemes. He also suggests the priority for different schemes.

Proposals received from these departments are then considered in detail by the Executive Committee at the district level. The officer of the planning department who keeps liaison with the district planning process is also associated with the work of the small team at the district level. The team examines the proposals of the department. Keeping in view : (1) the financial ceiling indicated by government, (2) the requirement of continuing and inevitable extension programmes, and (3) the guidelines issued by the planning department as also by the Administrative Departments/Heads of Departments. As regards the works programme like minor irrigation, medium irrigation, roads, water supply etc. the DPDC decides upon the priorities between different works on the basis of the suggestions received from the Executive Committee.

The plan approved by the Executive Committee is submitted to the Chairman, DPDC for review and suggestion who clears the plan within five to ten days. He makes suggestions on the plan in consultation with people's representatives. These suggestions are to be incorporated in the plan. In the month of November at the district level these proposals are again discussed by senior officers of the Planning Department with the Executive Committee and modifications/adjustments required to confirm to the guidelines and policies of the government are suggested for consideration of the DPDC. This meeting is held by the District Collector with the representatives of the State Planning Department or Deputy Secretary (Planning) and two to three under Secretaries. The main purpose of scrutinising the plan is to ensure the adherence to the commitment made to the Planning Commission in regard to MNP, SCP and other Central Government schemes.

The Draft Annual Plan examined by the senior officer of the Planning Department is then placed before the DPDC for approval in the month of December. The copies of the plan are supplied to the members of DPDC 10 days in advance along with agenda. The modifications if any approved by the DPDC are integrated in the draft Annual Plan.

By January 5, Draft Annual Plan is submitted by the Collector and Member-Secretary to the State Planning Department and also to other Administrative Departments and Heads of Departments/Agencies.

The Draft Annual Plan is then examined in the State Planning Department with reference to the relevance of the schemes to the policies and priorities of the Government and scrutiny notes are prepared. These scrutiny notes are discussed with the Executive Committee of the DPDC at the state level meetings presided over by the Minister of State for planning as the case may be. This meeting is attended by 7 to 8 members including Zilla Parishad Chairman, Chief Executive Officer, Zilla Parishad, Collector, 2 to 3 MLAs and 2 to 3 nominated members by the Caretaker Minister. The Finance Minister, the Finance Secretary, Planning Minister, Planning Secretary and Heads of Departments also attend this meeting and suggestions made by the sectoral heads are incorporated in this plan.

The Draft District Annual Plans after discussions at the state level meetings are then incorporated in the state's Annual Plan and forward to the Planning Commission and the Ministries of the Government of India. After the annual plan of the state is finalised after discussions in the Planning Commission, modifications approved by the Planning Commission are then incorporated in the district Annual Plans and they are also communicated to the Collector and Member-Secretary for incorporation in the District Annual Plan. The Planning Department then consolidates the sector-wise allocation for each district and gets the break-up for state level schemes and district level schemes. The final copy of each district booklet at the state level is placed in the assembly for vote and the district plan gets a separate recognition in the budget.

By 15th of April, the District Collector receives the plan and informs each department the allocation and approved schemes.

Implementation and Monitoring

The schemes are then taken up for implementation by the concerned departments. In order to ensure timely implementation of the plan, frequent review of the plan programmes at the district level is ensured through monthly meetings of the Executive Committee of the District Planning and Dev. councils.

ORISSA

Plan Formulation

In the state of Orissa, micro level plans are formulated at the district level. The State Government issue detailed guidelines for preparation of Annual Action Plan which are communicated to all members of the DPC. For planning purposes block wise data are collected. The items covered under this data inventory are: temperature and rainfall, irrigation, animal husbandry, forestry, fisheries, cooperation, education, medical and health, housing, water supply and sewerage, Harijan and social welfare, marketing and distribution, storage and godown. Village-wise data for different facilities like schools, post-offices, hospitals, banks, shops, stockman centre etc. have also been collected. The subject matter working groups on the basis of available information assess potentiality and level of utilisation of resources in the district. On the basis of these information and the felt need of the people gaps and shortfalls in various socio-economic facilities are identified. Various programmes implemented in the district are also reviewed. On the basis of these information the working groups draw up draft plan for concerned sectors.

The working groups while formulating the annual action plan also keep in view the inter sectoral linkages. In case it is necessary joint meetings of different working groups, these are also organised to facilitate linking up of different sectoral plans. While formulating the plans the working groups are also required to make provision for the ongoing schemes on priority basis and to suggest new schemes on the basis of availability of funds.

The district planning unit on receiving the draft plan from the working groups, synchronise it and then it is placed in the DPC for a detailed discussion. Then the plan is submitted to District Planning Board for its approval. The approved district plans are supposed to be received by the State Government by 15th September so that the state plan is finalised on that basis (Table 5.2).[12] The Govt. of Orissa is contemplating to incorporate district plans in the state budget from 1989-90.

Table 5.2
Time Schedule for Plan Formulation in Orissa

Programme	Work completion date
1. Plan to be prepared by the working groups	30th June
2. Scrutiny at District planning unit and integration of the sectoral plans prepared by the working groups	31st July
3. Discussion in the DPC and preparation of draft plan	5th August
4. Placing before the district development Board for discussion and comments and its finalisation	31st Autust
5. Forwarding the plan to the concerned Heads of Departments and planning and cooperation dept.	15th September
6. Scrutiny in the respective Heads of Departments and integration with sectoral plan and submission to planning and cooperation department.	15th September
7. Integration with state plan in planning and cooperation department after due scrutiny as per guidelines of planning Commission.	31st October

UTTAR PRADESH
Plan Formulation

The State of Uttar Pradesh has the practice of formulating micro level plans through the district level officers of the concerned departments keeping in view the guidelines received from their line departments at the state level and also the financial allocation for their sector indicated to them. The different steps followed in plan formulation at the district level are as follows:

1. Formulation of the major objectives of district plan;
2. Compilation of data for district planning;
3. Bringing out the profile of the district in relation to the basic objectives;
4. Formulation of main strategy and thrust of district planning;
5. Analysis of the existing programmes and projects with reference to the strategy outlined above and proposals regarding;
   (a) modification of the on-going programmes and projects
   (b) inclusion of new projects and plans
   (c) interlinkages between various projects and programmes.
6. Assessment of resources for various programmes and projects.
7. A statement of physical and financial component of the plan.

The District plans so formulated and approved by District planning and Monitoring Committee as well as Divisional Committees, are examined at the state level with the help of concerned administrative departments which carry it to the state budget. After the budget is passed by the State Legislature, the financial sanctions are issued. In 1982-83, the sanctions were issued to the district level officers through respective heads of departments. But from 1983-84 the administrative departments issue financial sanctions direct to the district level officer with an intimation to the Head of the Department.

Implementation and Monitoring

The sectoral officers at the district level are incharge of implementation of the plan projects. Overall coordination of the implementation is done by the District Collector. The responsibility of review and monitoring of the progress of programme implementation also lies with the District Collector. He is assisted in this task by the D.D.O.

WEST BENGAL

Planning Process

In West Bengal plans are prepared at the district as well as block levels. Thus the district development plan document consists of plan for block and district sector schemes.

In the first year of Seventh Plan the block and Municipal level plans were prepared on the basis of the local needs which resulted in a plan size which exceeded the available fund. Drawing a lesson from this experience, from the second year of the Seventh Plan the procedure has been revised so as to take care of this aspect. The sectoral heads now indicate the flow of funds to the districts from their plan budget, assuming a growth rate of 5 per cent over the current year's level. While indicating flow of funds the departments set aside a part of the plan budget of their district and state level projects which are non-divisible outlay to be retained by the departments at the state level itself.

The district level departmental officers on receiving the tentative allocation figure from their line departments in consultation with the district planning committee further disaggregate the sectoral allocation for blocks and district level schemes.

The sectoral officers then send proposals for their sector and while doing so also indicate the tentative cost estimate of the schemes. Different alternative schemes as well as prioritisation of the schemes are also suggested by the sectoral officers.

The 'Parikalpana-O-Unnayan Asthayee Samithy' in all the blocks have completed the exercise of surveying mouzawise physical resources available within the block. On the basis of the analysis of the survey, the 'Parikalpana-O-Unnayan Asthayee Samithy' identifies feasible schemes in the area keeping in view the resource potentiality and advises the block planning committee on the selection of schemes to be incorporated in the block development plan.[13] Thus the technical aspect of the schemes identified is taken care of by Parikalpana-O-Unnayan Asthayee Samithy whereas BPC is left with the power of exercising its selection of choice. While selecting the schemes the BPC also takes care of the budgetary limit as well as the social need so as to maximise gains within the outlay limit. After selection of schemes pertaining to various sectors the BPC compiles a draft block plan and submit it to the district planning committee, endorsing a copy to different district level officers.

The district level officers simultaneously work on their inter-block and district level schemes keeping in view the outlay indicated to them. In consultation with the district planning committee they fix up the priority of the proposed schemes.

Once the exercise of prioritisation of inter-block and district level scheme is over, these are integrated with the block plan schemes pertaining to respective sectors. This compiled plan becomes the sectoral plan of the district which is submitted to the district planning committee which considers different aspects of these sectoral plans and accords tentative approval and permission for its submission to the Heads of departments at the state level.

At the same time, the district planning committee with its planning machinery integrates the block plan, municipal development plan, area/notified authority plans and other interblock and district level schemes into a draft district plan. The District planning committee also prepares an outlay matrix for each sector indicating the sources of fund including cooperative institution and banks. The district planning committee also takes into consideration the funds available from the Central Government schemes like IRDP, NREP, RLEGP, DPAP etc. and the schemes pertaining to these programmes are also integrated with the district development plan. These district plans are then discussed with the State Planning Board to integrate the district plan with that of the state level plan.

Monitoring and Evaluation

The task of monitoring of the district plan is discharged by a committee through frequent meetings, wherein the implementing officers appraise the progress of work and the difficulties in execution if any. The district planning committee sorts out the problem at their level such cases which require action by the state level officers, the matter is referred to them.

Concurrent evaluations are also occasionally conducted by the Sabhadhipathi, Zilla Parishad and the District Magistrate to know the flow of benefits to the target groups. The evaluation, monitoring and manpower directorate under development and planning department normally takes up evaluation studies and the findings of these studies are communicated to DPCs and concerned BPCs.

Conclusion

To sum up it can be said that by and large formulation of micro level plans are the responsibility of the sectoral officers at the district level who have to operate within the guidelines prescribed by the state level and the financial ceiling indicated. The draft plan so formulated is modified at different levels for its approval. The plan schemes are implemented by the sectoral officers which is monitored generally in monthly meeting held at the district level.

Notes and References

1. Lakshminarayana, S., op. cit., pp. 5-6.
2. Lakshminarayana, S., op. cit., pp. 7-8.
3. Barua, Bhaskar, op. cit., p. 1.
4. Govt. of Gujarat, op. cit., p. 361.
5. Giridhar, C.B., op. cit., p. 8.
6. Giridhar, C.B., op. cit., p. 14.
7. Kumar Ajit, op. cit., p. 7.
8. Kumar Ajit, op. cit., p. 6.
9. Govt. of Kerala, Special component plan proposals for scheduled castes, 1988-89, State Planning Board, Trivandrum, pp. 7-8.
10. Govt. of Kerala, Special component plan for scheduled castes, 1987-88, State Planning Board, Trivandrum, pp. 4-5.
11. Rajan, M.P., op. cit., p. 6.
12. Govt. of Orissa, op. cit., 2.
13. Sarkar, Bikaram, op. cit.

VI

Summary and Conclusions

In view of the glaring socio-economic disparities and hetrogenity in natural endowment the significance of micro level planning as a mechanism to ensure alround balanced development have been recognised from the very inception of planning process in the country and consistently advocated from one plan to another. In the first five year plan itself importance of micro planning at the district level within the framework of state plan was emphasised. It was carried further during the second five year plan and certain activities to be planned and executed at the district level were identified. The third plan emphasised the importance of micro level planning and the states were suggested to draw up plans adopting blocks and districts as planning units.

Inspite of all these efforts, during the fourth plan it was realised that the micro level planning has not taken off and the prevalent practice of formulating plan at the state level have not been able to take care of the diverse conditions existing in different pockets in the states. It, was, therefore, considered necessary to look in greater detail into the aspirations and requirements of specific areas, communities and situations and identify suitable measures for meeting these so as to draw maximum advantage of existing resource potentiality and local initiative. It was therefore, advocated again that micro level plans at the district level should be formulated, as the departmental officials who could formulate schemes suitable to local conditions were available at this level. It was, however, emphasised that national and state priorities should be kept in view while formulating plans for the districts and wherever necessary these would be supplemented by regional, sub-regional, market area and block plans for specific activities or functions.

In oder to facilitate planning at the micro level, Planning Commission took the initiative and evolved guidelines for plan formulation. The schemes which could be taken up for planning and execution at the district level were also listed out. The guidelines issued by the Planning Commission on district planning were suggestive and advisory in character and the state governments had the freedom to adopt or modify it according to their requirements.

As most of the states could not detail out these modalities, micro level planning was not operationalised. This necessitated strengthening of the planning machinery particularly at the state level to work out these modalities for micro level planning. With this end in view, the Planning Commission launched a scheme for strengthening of the regional/district planning units in the state planning departments with competent and qualified technical staff.

Since the beginning of the fifth Five-year Plan, problems like poverty, unemployment and social inequality received greater attention and became central themes of planning process. In order to deal with these situations, it was felt necessary to bring down the mechanism of planning and decision making to levels where they can come into grips with the people and their problems and planners can evolve appropriate package of programmes/activities with a measure of active community support. In response to the need of the situation, a number of special area development programmes were initiated and specialised agencies were constituted for their implementation. Moreover, for the implementation of anti-poverty and area based programmes, for provision of basic minimum needs, creation of employment opportunities etc. the need for decentralising planning efforts came to be increasingly felt. Therefore, at this stage, block level planning was conceived as a tool for accelerated development of rural areas through optimum utilisation of local resources for employment and income generation, on the one hand, and proper attention to local problems on the other. It was believed that a development block would be an ideal unit for planning and implementation of programmes by virtue of their relatively small area and population size, 'to enable intimate contact and understanding between the planners, those responsible for implementation of the programmes and the people'. Thus during 1978-79 200 blocks in the country were selected for plan formulation and this was extended to all the blocks in the country in 1980.

Although a block plan originally was conceived as a comprehensive plan to be formulated based on an assessment of local resource endowments and felt needs of the people, its coverage was limited to beneficiary oriented programmes and employment generating schemes. The ostensible reason for formulating the limited scope block plan was the lack of competent and qualified technical staff at block level. Keeping in view the dearth of qualified persons and lack of expertise in micro level planning it was decided to have a planning cell at the district level for formulation of block plans. Reviews made at the beginning of the sixth plan revealed that capabilities for micro level planning had still to be built up. The right procedure and suitable structures had to be evolved. In this direction, the working group on District Planning in 1982 advocated a gradual step by step approach. As a follow up the Planning Commission attempted building these support and procedures for effecting functional, financial and administrative decentralisation to the districts were outlined to the states. In response to this, many states took steps to disaggregate the divisible outlays of the state plans to district segment and introduced corresponding administrative decentralisation measures. A central scheme of strengthening the planning machinery at the district level was also launched and training on formulation of district and block plans was also imparted to selected officers.

Inspite of these efforts in the past five-year plans, the Seventh Plan observed that lack of adequate machinery for decentralised planning and administration continued to be a critical weakness in the existing system whereas with the introduction of a variety of new programmes for rural development, requiring close coordination with other departmental programmes in the rural areas, the need for decentralisation of planning and development administration to the district and block levels became all the more imperative. Therefore, in the current plan various measures are being adopted by Planning Commission to promote micro level planning in the country. As the deficiency in the existing machinery for micro level planning is quite evident the scheme for its strengthening is being continued. In addition to this, training needs in micro level planning for different target groups are being identified and strategy to achieve it is being evolved by a task force. Pending the task force report on an adhoc basis training programmes on formulation of micro level plans are also organised. In addition, Planning Commission is also providing technical guidance to staff of selected districts through Pilot projects on District Planning, to improve methodology and procedure for plan formulation. Under these Pilot projects five districts in the country namely, Tirunelvelli-Kattabomman (Tamil Nadu), Nashik (Maharashtra), Munger (Bihar) Sitapur (Uttar Pradesh), Shimla (Himachal Pradesh) are selected and micro level plans are being prepared under the technical guidance of NRD, Hyderabad. Besides this, district plans on pilot basis are being formulated for 17 districts in the states of Andhra Pradesh, Assam, Bihar, Himachal Pradesh, J & K, Karnataka, Kerala and Uttar Pradesh.

Efforts are being made to strengthen data base for natural resources inventory at the district level through use of remote sensing techniques and 100 districts have been selected for this purpose. Detailed land use maps are being prepared under this project for the selected districts. Besides, the use of computers in micro level planning is also being emphasised. The Department of Science and Technology has taken up a project called Natural Resources Data Management System (NRDMS) to develop computer compatible methodology for collection, storage analysis and retrieval of data on natural resources and socio-economic parametres. With this background we summarise here the status of diffferent aspects of micro level planning across the states.

Planning Machinery

Availability of institutional infrastructure for shouldering the responsibility of plan formulation and implementation is an important pre-requisite for micro level planning. As mentioned earlier eventhough in recognition of the necessity for proper institutional infrastructure, a scheme to strengthen it, was launched as early as the Fourth Five-year Plan, still the states are at different stages and have adopted varying patterns. Inspite of the prevailing diversity in the arrangements, there are some common features in the structure of planning machinery. This common feature is the existence of two tier agencies at the district level in most of the states responsible for plan formulation. One agency plays mainly an advisory role whereas the other one which may be called second tier planning machinery is an executive body and hence technical in nature.

The advisory body has different nomenclatures in different states like District Development and Review Board, District Planning Board, District Planning and Development Committee/District Planning and Development Council, etc. The state of Assam is an exception where this body exists only at the sub-divisional level which is known as sub-divisional planning and development council. These are high power bodies at the district level involving top level officials and elected representatives of the people in the district. In some states like Jammu and Kashmir, Kerala, Rajasthan and Nagaland the District Collector is the Chairman of this planning body whereas in all other states a Minister of the state cabinet is its Chairman.

District level heads of all developmental departments are ex-officio members of district level planning body. In addition to Government officials non-official members are also nominated in different states. In Bihar, President of the District Central Cooperative Bank, representatives from Lead Bank, Regional Development Corporation and other financing agencies are also included as ex-officio members. Further, people's representatives such as MLAs, MPs, MLC, Presidents of Taluka Boards, Zilla Parishads and District Panchayats are also nominated as members. This facilitates people's participation through their elected representatives. In Jammu and Kashmir, the entire members of cabinet are associated in district planning and development bodies and in Meghalaya, Nagaland and Punjab, a large number of prominent members of the area are also enrolled as members of district level planning body.

The district advisory body under reference, with all the district administrative machinery under its control, is mainly responsible for approval, sanction and review of plan and non-plan schemes implemented in the district. Other responsibilities of this body are to ensure (a) accelerated and balanced regional development of both rural as well as urban areas, (b) to indicate inter-sectoral priorities to the government for allocation of funds to different schemes implemented by various agencies at the district level (c) to allocate funds received from the State Government among various implementing agencies in the district, keeping in view the guidelines issued by the government from time to time, and (d) to accord administrative sanctions for individual schemes to be taken up from out of the funds so allocated. In Assam the sub-divisional planning and Development council also approves sites of different projects and list of beneficiaries.

Zilla Parishad

In some of the states three tier system of panchayat raj set up exists. In Andhra Pradesh and Karnataka the ZPP is another body constituted at the district level. The Chairman, ZPP is directly elected by all the voters in the district excluding those residing in municipal areas. All the Mandal Praja Parishad Presidents who are elected in the lower tier of panchayati raj system are the members of ZPP. In addition some Members from minorities and women are co-opted as members. The ZPP has jurisdiction over the entire rural areas in the district. In Karnataka ZPP is vested with planning and implementation of development programmes at the district level and has all the freedom to expend allocation to the district.

Executive Committee

In most of the states the district planning advisory body is assisted by an executive committee at the district level which is a compact body. In Bihar for example, this committee is headed by the Divisional Commissioner, in Gujarat by District Collector, whereas in Maharashtra, the designated Minister of the state is the head of this committee. Other members of the executive committee are District Development Commissioner, District Planning officer, the sectoral heads and representatives of district lead bank. In Gujarat it has a representative character built into it by the inclusion of the MLA from the district.

The executive committee plays a very pivotal role. The committee scrutinises the financial estimates of different schemes proposed in the plan and also ensures that these are in accordance with the guidelines issued by the government. In Bihar it also fixes the priority, goals and objectives of development at the district level. In Maharashtra, it has all powers of the DPDC and can discharge all functions of DPDC. In the state of U.P. the executive committee at the district level is called 'Pariyojana Rachanavan Abayutan Samithi' which also has to arrange for institutional finance for the implementation of IRDP and other schemes. It also ensures coordination between state sector and district level schemes so as to avoid duplication of effort. The 'Core Group' in

Assam at the district level is responsible for preparation of draft sub-divisional plans. It also scrutinises the operational plan submitted by the district heads of development departments. In Karnataka there are Standing Committees on finance and audit, planning and development, public works and amenities, social justice, education, agriculture and animal husbandry, health and industries. These are infact executive committees. In West Bengal also there are Standing Committees at the Z.P. as well as Panchayat Samithi levels known as Parikalpa-O-Unnayam. This committee undertakes resource survey and assists in formulating plan for the district. There are also working groups at the district level for reviewing the progress of development plan.

District Planning Cell/Unit—The task of Executive Committee is facilitated by the Planning Cell/unit at the district level. A review of the organisational structure available in district planning in different states has revealed that 17 states in the country have established Planning Cell at the district level with varying pattern and composition. In the state of Tamil Nadu only in three districts the planning cells have been constituted whereas in Rajasthan the District Planning officer is attached to DRDA. These district planning cells have very limited staff and in most cases consist of a Chief Planning officer/District Planning officer, assisted by statistical and research assistants and clerical staff. The Chief Planning officer is invariably from statistical background except in Kerala and Gujarat where officers from Indian Administrative Service and other state services are also inducted to this post. The officers in the planning cells by and large do not have any qualifications in planning. Even though this is supposed to be a technical cell, the functions being discharged by this cell are only compilation of planning proposals received from sectoral officers and rendering assistance to District Planning Board/Committee in its routine monitoring of the progress of implementation of the plan projects.

State Level Planning Cell

In the states of Assam, Bihar, Maharashtra and Kerala, a cell/division has been created under the State Planning and Development Department/Board, to formulate policies, procedures and guidelines for preparation of micro level plans and to work out norms for distribution of funds among the sub-divisions and fixations of size of the annual plans. By and large the state level planning machinery has a supervisory role.

A close look on the availability of institutional infrastructure at different states in the country leads to the conclusion that the states have succeeded in making some arrangements for planning at the district level in most of the states. In some of the states at sub-divisional, block and mandal levels, process of micro level planning has been started. The long list of functions assigned to different advisory bodies as well as executive and technical units reflect only the importance of these institutions. But these institutions have to go a long way to have the technical capabilities to discharge the duties assigned to them in the most fruitful way.

Functional Decentralisation

For operationalisation of micro planning, identification of schemes and activities to be planned and implemented at the district level and below is very crucial. This necessitates defining the scope of the micro level plan explicitly to make it clear to the planning and implementing agencies their real roles, leaving no scope for confusion and duplication in their role performance. Moreover, the quantum of fund to be earmarked for plan implementation at district level and below have also to be decided on the basis of the schemes to be taken up at these levels.

It may be noted that out of 21 states who have accepted the concept of micro level planning only 15 states have identified schemes for planning at micro level. These however, differ from state to state. The states like Bihar, Gujarat, Maharashtra, Orissa, Uttar Pradesh have identified district sector schemes whereas the state of Assam has gone a step ahead in functional decentralisation and has identified sub-divisional level schemes. There are also states like Madhya Pradesh and West Bengal which have listed out block level schemes whereas Andhra Pradesh and Karnataka have mandal level schemes also. Inspite of this diversity, except Assam, most of the states have categorised district sector schemes. The basic principle followed in the identification of the district sector schemes is that the schemes' benefits would be confined to the district. Similarly the schemes which benefit more than one district, irrespective of their location are categorised as state sector schemes. Thus schemes like major and medium irrigation, major industries, state highways, power generation, university education are outside the purview of micro level planning and fall under the category of state sector scheme whereas schemes like agicultural production and minor irrigation, soil conservation, animal husbandry, forestry, horticulture, small scale industry, primary and secondary education, district and village roads, rural electrification, rural water supply and sanitation, health, rural housing, social welfare, and cooperation etc. are of relevance to individual districts and hence are classified under district sector schemes.

Gujarat has classified the district level schemes based on the type of fund available for taking up the schemes at the district level and below. Thus the schemes admissible under discretionary outlays, incentive outlays and schemes not admissible under discretionary and incentive outlays have been listed out.

The point which emerges out of the cross country analysis of the schemes listed out as State, District, Sub-division, Block/Taluka and Mandal level is that the items included vary from state to state. If the classification of schemes and sectors is made strictly on the basis of technical feasibility of its planning and implementation at different levels, there is not much scope for this diversity among different states. It leads to the conclusion that there is scope for further revision and reclassification of schemes on the basis of rational analyses. In some states justification given for retaining certain schemes at the state level is that it requires constant technical supervision. At this stage of development, it may be a right step but as the competence of the implementing agencies at the local level increases, out of their experience, even such activities can be safely passed on to the local agencies.

Devolution of Financial Resources

The disaggregation of state plan outlays for districts and other lower units on rational basis is quite essential for making micro level planning a fruitful exercise. The state governments have realised its importance and hence accepted the basic idea of disaggregation of state plan outlay into state sector outlay and district sector outlay.

It may be observed that the division of the state plan outlays into state and district sector outlays depend upon the number of schemes listed out at these levels. In general about 30-40 per cent of the total outlay of the state plan is earmarked for district sector schemes. In

Assam it is 20 per cent, Uttar Pradesh 30 per cent, Andhra Pradesh 40 per cent, Bihar, Gujarat, Kerala, 40 per cent, Maharashtra and Jammu and Kashmir 40-45 per cent. The district sector outlay so arrived at is redistributed among different districts on the basis of some variants of Gadgil formula. The common criteria of the allocation formula are—

1. Population
2. Population of SC/ST small farmers
3. Agriculture backwardness
4. Irrigation backwardness
5. Industrial backwardness
6. Communication backwardness
7. Drinking water problem
8. Others

Out of these, population is generally given a weightage of 50 to 60 per cent.

The outlay thus arrived at for each district is distributed among different sectors/sub-divisions/blocks/mandals as the case may be. In Assam 50 per cent of the district sector allocation is distributed to different sub-divisions. In Jammu and Kashmir, Kerala and West Bengal it is distributed among blocks and in Karnataka among mandals. This distribution is done on the basis of some approved norms.

Out of the district sector outlay about 80 per cent is generally reserved for the normal district level schemes approved by the State Planning departments and formulated as per the guidelines of the Central and State Governments. In most cases sectorwise allocation of the district fund is communicated by the State Planning Departments leaving little scope for the district level planning body to propose schemes and fix up its priority based on the local potentialities, problems and people's need. However in a number of states to provide some freedom to the district planning bodies some fund is kept aside to be utilised by the local agency for implementing schemes of local importance selected by them. These are discretionary outlays or untied fund. The amount earmarked as untied fund varies from State to State. It is Rs. 3 crores per district in Bihar and in Orisssa it is Rs. 25-30 lakhs per district. The states like Bihar, Himachal Pradesh, and Orissa distribute the untied fund among districts on the basis of certain formulae whereas in other states lumpsum amount is provided to districts under this head.

The concept of incentive outlay is in vogue in Andhra Pradesh, Gujarat and Jammu and Kashmir. The incentive outlays are allocated against some matching fund raised by the local agency for implementing schemes of their choice. This provides some freedom to the district planning bodies to reserve funds for implementing schemes of local importance selected by them. In Andhra Pradesh a lumpsum of Rs. 50 lakhs per district is provided as incentive outlay for the implementation of 'Telugu Grameena Kranti Patham' scheme. In Jammu and Kashmir also the allocation under this head is same. Gujarat has a different pattern and 50% of the total district sector allocated is reserved for incentive outlay and is distributed among talukas in the district on the basis of certain criteria.

In respect of discretionary and incentive outlays, the district planning bodies have freedom for selection and implementation of schemes of their choice. This can be considered as the first step in the devolution of financial power for local level planning.

Plan Formulation, Implementation and Monitoring

Currently in most of the states at the micro level only Annual Action Plans are prepared. Even in the states of Assam, Jammu and Kashmir and Karnataka where sub-divisions, blocks and mandals respectively have been accepted as planning units, plan formulation exercise is confined to the district level. In Andhra Pradesh where mandals have been carved out as development units, plans for agriculture, sericulture, animal husbandry etc. are formulated at the state level and plans for other sectors are prepared by the concerned district heads of departments. In Gujarat, schemes to be implemented with the discretionary and incentive outlays are chalked out by the Taluka planning committees which is finalised by the District Planning Boards whereas planning for the normal district sector schemes are dealt with by the concerned sectoral officers at the district level. In West Bengal while the district level sectoral officers formulate plan for district level schemes, the 'Parikalpana-o-unayan Asthayee Samithi' (block level standing committee) identifies feasible schemes for the blocks to be incorporated by the block planning committee in the block development plan.

The Annual Action Plan proposals so formulated are scrutinised at the district level by an executive body. In Assam, scrutiny of plan proposals is done by a core group at the district level while in Gujarat the Executive Planning Committee scrutinises plan proposals. In Karnataka district planning unit is incharge of scrutiny while in Kerala the working groups scrutinise plan proposals. In Maharashtra, the District Planning Unit, Executive Committees and State Planning Departments scrutinise the plan proposals while in Orissa, the working groups scrutinise the plan proposals.

In Bihar plan proposals are received from sectoral heads, MLAs, MPs, block Pramukhs and BDOs by the District Planning Cell and the priority of different proposed schemes is fixed up by the District Magistrate and in West Bengal by District Planning Committee.

In most cases the plan is approved at the district level are forwarded to Government for final approval. In Assam sub-divisional planning and development council gives plan approval. In Andhra Pradesh it is the District Planning and Review Board which approves the plan. Similarly in Bihar it is by District Planning and Development Council, in Gujarat and Jammu and Kashmir by District Planning Board, in Karnataka by Zilla Parishad, in Kerala by District Advisory Committee for SC (only special component plan), in Madhya Pradesh by District Planning Boards, in Maharashtra by District Planning and Development Council, in Orissa by District Planning Board, in Uttar Pradesh by District Planning and Monitoring Committee and in West Bengal by District Planning Committee. In the case of Karnataka the Zilla Parishad is vested with powers to accord final sanction.

The plan formulation exercise generally starts in the month of August and the draft plan is submitted to the district level authority within two months. In Bihar plan formulation commences in the month of August/September. In Orissa the departments are required to submit their draft plan by the end of June.

As regards implementation of the plan schemes, it is invariably undertaken by the district level departments as per the guidelines and directions received from the state headquarters. In Andhra Pradesh the beneficiary oriented programmes and schemes of different agencies and corporations are implemented through mandal praja parishad. In Karnataka the plan is implemented by the sectoral officers at the district level with the help of mandal level officers. All the activities of the Zilla Parishad are implemented through 9 standing committees. In Madhya Pradesh 'Janapath Panchayats' are responsible for the implementation of certain schemes related to Agriculture, Forestry, Animal Husbandry, Public Works, Engineering Education, Social Welfare and Cooperation. The implementation of these schemes are taken up by the concerned departments.

The progress of implementation of the plan schemes are monitored at different levels. In Assam monthly meetings of district development body are held for monitoring as well as to ensure inter-departmental coordination in plan implementation. Even the sub-divisional planning and development council is required to monitor the progress of implementation at least twice a year. In Andhra Pradesh District Development and Review Board monitors the plan implementation. In Bihar the implementation of Annual Action Plan is discussed in the monthly meetings of the DPDC and the departments are also required to furnish their monthly progress reports. In Gujarat the District Planning Board monitors progress of implementation of Minimum Needs and Poverty alleviation programmes. Executive planning committee, District Planning Officer as well as State Planning Department also monitor the progress.

In Himachal Pradesh the state government has fixed norms for utilisation of funds under the plan schemes for each quarter of the financial year. The progress reports of financial and physical content of plan schemes are reviewed in the quarterly meetings of the District Planning and Development Committee. In Jammu and Kashmir review of implementation of Annual Plans is done by the state cabinet along with sectoral officers in the districts. In Karnataka monitoring and review of the development activities are taken up by different departments, mandals and planning units. The progress reports received by the planning units are placed in the Zilla Parishad monthly review meetings. In Maharashtra regular reviews of the implementation of plan programmes at the district level is ensured through monthly meetings of the executive committee of the district planning and development council.

Thus it can be seen that micro level planning is only a periodical exercise and by and large, perspective plans are not drawn up. The plan formulation is undertaken by the sectoral departments and compiled by the Executive Planning Committees or district planning units and placed in the district planning boards. The plan implementation is undertaken through the respective departments except some of the beneficiary oriented and employment generation schemes which are implemented at the Taluka/block/mandal levels. Monitoring of implementation of schemes is undertaken through periodical review meetings held under the auspices of District Planning and Development Boards with the exception of Karnataka where it is reviewed by Zilla Parishad and in Jammu and Kashmir by the State cabinet in addition to the regular reviews in the District Development Board. Nevertheless a project approach and an in built system for periodical monitoring and applying corrective measures is lacking in the micro level plans formulated by almost all the States.

The history of planning since independence in the country is adorned by several bold experiments. Micro level planning is one among the many in the list. Nevertheless it is heartening to note that 21 States in the country have accepted this concept and have constituted district level advisory bodies. Out of these States 17 have gone one step ahead and have also established district planning cells.

The fact cannot be denied that it is a major achievement and it is evident that the stage is set, in these states, for formulation of micro level plans. But one point which has to be also borne in mind is the poor capability of the agency or the existing set up to handle this technical task of planning. As a micro level plan is required to respond to the local problems, to take care of the local requirements, and also make proper use of the available limited resources through productive processes, the exercise of planning at this level is a complicated and a challenging exercise. It was assessed as early as in 1977 by Prof. Dantwala that there is hardly any skill available at the block level for micro level planning. The situation has not improved much since then, and it will not be an exaggeration to say that the technical know-how or skill for plan formulation is yet to percolate below the state level in most of the cases. It was envisaged that the district planning team will formulate perspective and Annual Action Plan for the area but in practice this task is not attended to by any district planning team in the country. The main function of this team is to collect the plans prepared by the sectoral officers, compile it, examine it against the financial allocations made for these sectors and schemes and also to collect the progress report from the implementing agencies. Thus the planning team is meant only for non planning work and the expectation that the formulation of scientific micro level plans will be facilitated by establishing the planning team so constituted is a myth.

Inspite of these organisational arrangements, still it is the sectoral officers who are responsible for chalking out the plan schemes on the basis of the guidelines received from the State Planning Department or Heads of Departments as well as the fund available for their sectors. The data base required for plan formulation available with these officers are inadequate and the officer concerned has no choice but to go by his subjective judgement and past experience. In the absence of detailed area/location wise information on resource potentiality of different sectors, the officers are not in a position to go beyond listing out of schemes irrespective of their feasibility, and just indicate the fiancial requirements of these schemes. Moreover, the locations at which these schemes can be taken up on priority basis do not form part of the plan. Thus the plan so prepared is devoid of the spatial feature which is an important component of micro level plan. These plans also do not reflect the felt need of the people.

The plan proposals thus arrived at are just compiled as a comprehensive plan and placed before the District Planning Body for approval. It is at this stage that the people's participation in planning through peoples representatives (who are supposed to be people's spokesmen) is ensured. As a ritual some suggestions are made at this stage and some minor modifications are also made. The plan is then reviewed at the state level and undergoes some prunity keeping in view the financial constraints. Thus, the prevalent system is not conducive for producing "micro level plan". It is a plan formulated in isolation by the sectoral officers on the basis of the guidelines worked out at the State level within the financial ceiling indicated, without peoples participation, ignoring integrated planning approach and also omitting spatial allocation of resources.

The review of the current-status of micro level planning in the country pinpoints the need to take up the following measures for projecting micro level planning in the country. These are:

Improved Data Base

In order to formulate realistic plans on scientific lines at the micro level, the first pre-requisite is strengthening of data base. To start with socio-economic information should be gathered and maintained adopting village as the basic unit. The natural resource inventory showing the distribution pattern, level of utilisation along with potentiality for future development is essential for identification of schemes.

Strengthening of Planning Cell

As the sectoral proposals are drawn in isolation by the officers of concerned departments it is necesary that these proposals are properly reexamined and integrated to make them realistic and derive optimum return from these schemes. This necessitates deployment of officers trained in Regional Planning/Area Planning in the planning cells to perform this task in an efficient way.

The second important role of the District Planning Cell would be formulation of "Spatial Plan" to translate the socio-economic plan into location specific action plans. The spatial plan is also a tool for physical integration of different schemes. As there is no sectoral department to deal with this aspect, the District Planning Cell has to take care of it. This is a specialised job and would require the services of a trained planner. It is in this context that the Planning Commission has suggested a spatial planner as a member of the planning team to be appointed on priority basis.

Training of Sectoral Officers

The sectoral officers will continue to be the main instruments for project identification even after strengthening the district planning cell. Hence in order to improve the quality of plan formulation, the sectoral officers need to be trained in the methods and techniques of plan formulation. Their training should have two components. First they should be exposed to the aspects of comprehensive development plan like concept, components and steps. The second part of the training should be on plan formulation for the concerned sectors.

Formulation of Perspective Development Plan

By and large currently planning process is limited to formulation of annual action plans. But for determining the scope of development in different sectors and to fix up the priority of implementation of different schemes a perspective development plan reflecting resource potential of the area is a basic requirement. This will facilitate to foresee the requirements of different activities and areas and enable to take advance action to meet these requirements.

Index

[illegible] I [illegible] punish-
[illegible] in a party controversy, is
[illegible] experienced in
[illegible] their
[illegible] danger
comprising [illegible]

Romesh [illegible]